the
introvert
& extrovert
in love

making it
work when
opposites
attract

MARTI OLSEN LANEY, PSY.D., MFT
MICHAEL L. LANEY

New Harbinger Publications, Inc.

Publisher's Note

This publication is designed to provide accurate and authoritative information in regard to the subject matter covered. It is sold with the understanding that the publisher is not engaged in rendering psychological, financial, legal, or other professional services. If expert assistance or counseling is needed, the services of a competent professional should be sought.

Distributed in Canada by Raincoast Books

Copyright © 2007 by Marti Olsen Laney and Michael L. Laney
New Harbinger Publications, Inc.
5674 Shattuck Avenue
Oakland, CA 94609
www.newharbinger.com

Cover and text design by Amy Shoup; Acquired by Melissa Kirk; Edited by Karen O'Donnell Stein

---

Library of Congress Cataloging-in-Publication Data

Laney, Marti Olsen.
  The introvert and extrovert in love : making it work when opposites attract / Marti Olsen Laney and Michael L. Laney.
    p. cm.
  ISBN-13: 978-1-57224-486-3 (pbk.)
  ISBN-10: 1-57224-486-0 (pbk.)
  1. Typology (Psychology) 2. Interpersonal relations. 3. Love. I. Laney, Michael L. II. Title.
BF698.3.L363 2007
158.2'4--dc22

                               2006102710

FSC
Mixed Sources
Product group from well-managed
forests and other controlled sources
Cert no. SW-COC-002283
www.fsc.org
© 1996 Forest Stewardship Council

11   10   09

10   9   8   7   6   5   4   3   2

table of contents

acknowledgments v

introduction
innies and outies aren't just belly buttons . . I

1   when opposites attract
    are you an innie or an outie? . . . . I I

2   all brains aren't the same
    innie and outie hardwiring I9

3   couple combinations
    play the music and dance 49

4 becoming bilingual
speaking innie and outie 71

5 to go or not to go?
that is the question. 93

6 pillow talk
uncovering intimacy 119

7 regaining balance & recharging
boosting batteries 137

8 the more things change . . .
adjusting to life 161

9 sticky wickets
when worlds collide. 181

10 harnessing your strengths
team up when stepping out. 197

references 217

acknowledgments

"In a successful marriage, there is no such thing as one's way. There is only the way of both, only the bumpy, dusty, difficult, but always mutual path." —Phyllis McGinley

Cultivating a book, like gardening, takes planning, planting, and pruning. It requires experienced horticulturists, nature, nurture, and sweat. First, we want to thank our editor, Melissa Kirk, who gave us the seeds of inspiration for the project. Her green thumb guided us when we needed to yank a few weeds, prune here and there, and add a stake or two to firm up the design. We approached the blank pages with trepidation, because this is our first cowriting effort. As the quote above suggests, it's been a bumpy, dusty, and difficult path. Like all successful introvert-extrovert couples, we managed to blend our skills and find a path we could walk together.

The book wouldn't have matured without help from a number of important people. We wish to thank Gail Libman and Valerie Hunter for adding sunlight, showers, and occasionally a dash of fertilizer. We are grateful to the introvert-extrovert couples who generously offered us their stories, secrets, and solutions. Marti treasures what she learns about human relationships from her clients, who opened their garden gates and let her into their private lives. We wish to acknowledge all the dedicated scientists around the world who study temperament, neuroscience, and human behavior. We also want to thank the editors, production staff, and marketing team at New Harbinger Publications who have helped with this book.

And last, we want to acknowledge you, the reader. Never forget that nature created introverts and extroverts for a reason. Cherish and enjoy your mutual paths. ♡

introduction
innies and outies aren't just belly buttons

"I want a divorce because we have absolutely nothing in common."
—spoken by Jane Fonda in the film <u>Barefoot in the Park</u>
(screenplay by Neil Simon)

Remember when you were a kid and you called belly buttons either "innies" or "outies"? Belly buttons tucked inside the tummy are often called "innies"; those that pop out for the entire world to see are named "outies." Temperaments (inborn patterns that last a lifetime), like navels, also come in two main types. They either turn inward and are referred to as "introverts," or "innies," or they face outward and are called "extroverts," or "outies." Innies gain energy from and enjoy reflecting on their internal thoughts and feelings. Outies gain energy out in the world and enjoy external activities and interaction.

The quote above is from Neil Simon's *Barefoot in the Park*, a film about newlyweds with differing personalities and interests. Extroverted Jane

Fonda wants a divorce because her introverted husband, played by Robert Redford, is too dull. She considers him a stick-in-the-mud because he won't loosen up enough to go barefoot in Central Park in the winter. By the close of the film, however, they learn to treasure their differences. After all, they have love in common.

Why We Wrote This Book

Dealing with the differences between innies and outies can be quite a challenge. Innies and outies come from two different worlds. Therefore, maintaining a bond often requires an interpreter. Because we tend to behave in and see the world so differently, so many people have asked, "How do you do it?" about our forty-one-year introvert-extrovert marriage. People also ask us about their partners' strange behavior: "Why do I have to blast her out of the house?" "Why doesn't he listen to me?" "Why does she clam up?" "Why can't she decide faster? Everything is 'Let me think about it.'" "Why does he always want to go out—can't we stay home for a change?" "Why do we have to visit *every* tourist attraction?" Innies and outies can be complete puzzles to each other.

These questions sparked the idea of our writing a book about innie and outie relationships. We have cultivated, sometimes the hard way, at least a few skills that have helped us maintain our marriage. We also researched and developed a few new skills while writing this book. Since the innie-outie match is one common type of partnering, these differences impact lots of couples. Extroverts help pull out innies, and innies usually are attracted to outies' "ideal" social skills. After more than forty years together we know *any* relationship has lots of thrills and chills. It's especially important for innie-outie couples to understand and appreciate the differences between them, and it's our hope that this book will help people do just that.

Why Are Differences in Temperament So Powerful?

Temperaments are consistent patterns of behavior in people. They shape our basic needs, core values, and natural talents. They influence our thoughts, feelings, actions, and individual responses to life situations. For example, research tells us that reactions during a crisis fall into two categories: some folks (innies) pause first and think, and others (outies) act first and think later (Keltikangas-Jarvinen et al. 1999). These are opposing reactions to the same event. Both responses promote survival. In another example of the impact of temperament on behavior, studies show that innies tend to step on the brakes when the traffic light turns yellow. Extroverts tend to gun it (Zuckerman 2004).

When romantic partners first meet, their introverted or extroverted temperament may not be apparent. And even if their temperaments are noticeable, in the honeymoon stage of a relationship differences are often seen as refreshing and exciting. However, as the initial glow fades, those *same* differences become tiresome and irritating. What started out as a romantic waltz turns into a slow-motion kickboxing match. As daily life sets in, opposing orientations crop up in all aspects of the relationship. Below are some examples of situations from our years together that reveal the widespread influence our temperaments have had on our lives.

SCHEDULING A WEEKEND

Marti has always hated jam-packed weekends. Nowadays, she only books one social gathering per weekend. Years ago, however, when our daughters were young, weekends jammed up quickly. Mike, on the other hand, likes a well-stocked calendar. One holiday season Mike sat down to fill Marti in on our upcoming engagements. His eyes sparkled; his face glowed in the reflection of his glossy calendar. "December 16 is my office party. Do you want to go? The seventeenth is our daughter's soccer game followed by the team's holiday pizza party. The eighteenth is the

McFineys' open house." Mike looked up at Marti with complete inno-
cence and said, "We owe the Smiths; what about inviting them for dinner
on the nineteenth?" Marti's head was spinning. She staggered toward
a chair. "That's the last straw," she managed to spurt out. "We need a
social engagement agreement, signed in blood."

ATTENDING A PARTY

Mike had planned a large rootin', tootin' cowboy-themed party at
Warner Brothers' Western back lot in Burbank that would attract a lot
of potential animators to the company's Feature Animation division.
Everyone would be armed with water pistols and could swagger down the
dusty "streets" like Gary Cooper preparing for a shootout in the movie
High Noon. The party was just getting started about nine o'clock in the
evening when Mike called Marti to try to persuade her to join him. "It's
a great party; come on over." "Sounds like you're having a great time,"
Marti said. The image of watching a bunch of rowdy strangers shooting each other with water pistols sounded less than enticing to her. And
it paled in comparison to her toasty bed, a mystery novel, and flannel
jammies. Mike phoned Marti again around ten o'clock and tried once
more to talk her into coming over, thinking, How could Marti pass this
great experience up? It never occurred to him that Marti was already
having a good time.

SHOPPING

We were snug as bugs in a Jane Austen—era manor house tucked
between rolling green hills in England's Lake District National Park.
While browsing in the manor's cozy shop, Marti fell in love with a set
of antique silver tea spoons nestled in a blue velvet case. Mike said, "Buy
them." Marti said, "Well, let me think about it." The next morning, as
we were leaving, she finally decided to buy them. "Closed Today," read

the sign hanging by a blue ribbon on the shop door. Marti was so disappointed and would pine for the spoons for the next ten years. Feeling annoyed, Mike said, "Why didn't you just buy them when you first saw them?"

VACATIONS

When our hotel room door slams shut, the vacation begins for Marti. She fills the tub, sprinkles in some bath salts, orders room service, checks out the skyline, and buys an in-room movie. She slips between the cool sheets and sinks back onto the crisp pillows. She sighs and relaxes—she is on vacation. Mike, on the other hand, is raring to go. First, he scouts out the hotel. He returns with a lilt in his step and a plethora of details to report. Mike gives Marti a blow-by-blow account of the hotel's features, and then he leaves again to explore the blocks around the hotel. When he comes back to give Marti his impressions of the local neighborhood and tell her his ideas about the next day's agenda, she's very likely already asleep.

SURPRISE PARTIES

Mike loves to throw surprise parties. On the night of the second surprise party he'd thrown for Marti, he led her to believe that they would be celebrating her birthday at a restaurant in Los Angeles. As they drove over the hill toward the lights of the city, Marti's tummy was growling because she had been saving calories for her birthday dinner. Approaching the restaurant after the half-hour drive, Mike said, "Oh my gosh. I forgot my wallet." Since Marti had only lip gloss and Kleenex in her purse, she knew we had to return home. Mike called home and asked the babysitter to see if his wallet was there (really to check if everyone was primed for our return). Marti was feeling faint from hunger by this time, and she was angry and frustrated that Mike had not checked for his wallet earlier.

We pulled into our driveway and he hopped out of the car. "Come on in," he said. "No, it will just take you a minute, Mike, so I'll just stay in the car," Marti said. "Grab some crackers for me while you're inside." In a flash he returned, without the crackers, and went over to her window. "You'd better come in. I think there's a water leak in the kitchen," he said. Marti scrambled out of the car and made tracks to the front door. She had barely opened the door when shouts of "Happy birthday" blasted her eardrums. She jumped about a foot off the floor. Jolts of adrenaline rattled her body. It took her several moments to realize that it was a surprise party. Although she did end up having fun, it took her days to recover from the surge of adrenaline. That night, after all the guests had left, Mike said he thought it was the best surprise party he had ever thrown. Marti shot him a serious glare and said, "Never again, if you want to stay married." There have been no more surprise parties.

Beneficial Differences

As you can see, and as you probably know from your own experiences, differences between innies and outies can easily switch from beneficial to detrimental. Overnight those once-attractive qualities turn into sources of irritation. Your partner displays behaviors that suddenly seem puzzling and frustrating. Finger pointing begins, and the relationship becomes stressed.

While interviewing couples, we have found that innies tend to think of outies as intrusive, loud, and demanding. Outies, on the other hand, think innies are slow, withholding, and mysterious. There is good news, however: opposing temperaments also bring complementary advantages that balance and strengthen relationships. For instance, most introverts tend to treasure their hearth and home. They savor quiet time cocooning with familiar and comfortable people. They value turning inward and spending time alone. Extroverts, on the other hand, tend to crave social events, stimulating environments, and lots of activity in the outside world. They value turning outward and taking action. Although these differences provide fertile ground for increased conflicts, they also provide balance and potential for growth. When each partner's differences are appreciated, they complement each other. Outies find themselves building a richer inner world, and innies find themselves gaining information and experience from the outside world.

What Does Science Say About Temperament?

We chose to address the topics in this book based on current scientific studies, comments received from readers of Marti's previous books on introversion, interviews with innie-outie couples, and some of our own personal experiences.

We have integrated sound scientific studies from numerous fields, such as temperament, neuroscience, and relationship research conducted all over the globe. We have woven together numerous studies in order to develop a complete physiological portrait of innie and outie temperaments. Technology has expanded our insight into our brains and bodies. Now we can lift the lid off the brain and see what's happening inside, rather like peering into the inner workings of a watch, allowing us to understand what makes innies and outies tick.

Scientists study the brain through various lenses. First, they look at brain scans. Regions of the brain light up, reflecting a high level of electrical activity, when the brain is burning energy. Scientists link these active brain regions with particular functions and behaviors. Second, they study brain-injured patients. Scientists map injured brain regions with their lost or impaired functions. Third, animals are studied, because we have the same basic brain structures as rats, dogs, monkeys, and chimps

(Dugatkin 2004). Fourth, scientists learn from the research done at twin study centers in Minnesota, Denmark, and other locations, which follow identical twins who have been raised apart, in order to shed light on the nature-versus-nurture debate. This research tells us that identical twins raised apart have striking similarities when they meet later in life. Meeting as adults, twins may find that they like using the same Swedish toothpaste, reading Superman comic books, laughing at the same jokes, and buying '56 Chevys to restore. But identical twins are never exactly alike. People of similar temperament (either introverts or extroverts), like identical twins, will show striking hardwired similarities, yet they will never be carbon copies of each other.

There Is More Than One Way to Read a Book

Each person's approach is valid. Stay curious about your similarities and differences as you read the chapters. And in today's world, finding time to read is easier said than done. Try reading just one chapter every week. Look over the table of contents and pick those topics you are interested in; check those out first. Set your kitchen timer for fifteen minutes and read a few pages. Have fun; be creative and playful as you read the book. Invite your partner to read the book with you.

An outie partner may not be as enthusiastic as an innie might be about this information. Most extroverts don't feel as if anything is wrong with them and don't feel that they need to change, since they represent the norm of Western society and outnumber introverts three to one (Myers and Myers 1995). As a result, outies may be reluctant to read this book. If this is the case, then see if you can help your partner discuss his or her reluctance (talking while driving or walking is sometimes more comfortable for outies than talking face to face). If your outie partner wants to read the book in bite-size pieces, that's okay, too, even though he or she may expect to be criticized for reading it this way. Or, if your outie is feeling blamed for the differences between you, invite him or her to skim chapter 2. Most people find the concept of hardwiring fascinating. Learning that our different styles are biologically and chemically based immediately reduces blame and shame.

Stay flexible. Perhaps you might want to read the whole book together on a weekend getaway. Or read it separately and then discuss it. You could take turns reading it aloud to each other (our favorite method), stopping to chat about issues that catch your attention. Or simply sit in the same room and read it silently together.

Our Hope for Your Relationship

It's okay to be an innie. It's okay to be an outie. But a relationship between such different people will cause a few relational bumps along the way. We hope this book helps to smooth out your road. When you both understand your brain and body's hardwiring, you will be paving the way toward reduced shame and guilt and increased acceptance. Your growing ability to appreciate each other's peculiarities will flatten those relational speed bumps. Of course, a few bumps can shake things up and help your relationship grow. Differences don't need to ruin your relationship; in fact, they can actually spice it up. In the chapters ahead we will discuss the secrets to a successful and intimate innie-outie relationship. We encourage you to celebrate your differences—they offer new ways to strengthen your relationship. ♡

I

when opposites attract

are you an innie or an outie?

"If we cannot now end our differences at least we can
help make the world safe for diversity."
—John F. Kennedy

Swiss psychoanalyst Carl Jung coined the terms "introversion" and "extroversion" (though he actually spelled the latter term
"extraversion"), believing that these temperaments were extremely crucial
to our ability to understand interpersonal relationships (Liberty 2002).
Jung thought temperamental differences were like chemicals: when mixed,
both are transformed. Of course, in this mixing process they either blend
together smoothly like milk and chocolate or remain separate like oil and
water. Some mixes may actually erupt in explosions. People with opposite
temperaments have the potential to appreciate, transform, and improve
one another. Or they can explode in exasperation, fights, and rejection.
In this chapter we'll be examining the evolution of temperaments, the

origins of introversion and extroversion, and the reasons opposites are attracted to each other.

Opposites Do Attract

Why do opposites attract? Evolutionary psychologists believe that one reason we find partners who are different from ourselves is to spice up our gene pool. Our chances of survival as a species increase if we sniff out a partner with genetic strengths we don't possess. We're not kidding about sniffing out partners, either. We can actually smell a date's immune system (Slater 2006). If it's different from ours we may begin to feel the stirrings of love. If the relationship produces a child, the blending of both immune systems increases the child's chances of survival. Another reason that opposites attract is the opportunity to learn new skills from a partner with a different background or abilities. The last and most important reason is that partnering outside our "clan" allows us to appreciate and adapt to people who are not related to us. This is beneficial because we must continue to grow and stretch our abilities to adapt to an ever-changing world.

Philosophers and scientists have been sorting people and their behaviors into categories for more than twenty-five centuries. From the earliest times, people who attempted to describe human behaviors noticed two main patterns. One pattern was a tendency to be "ingoing" and reflective. The other was a tendency to be outgoing and active. Obviously they were on to something, because being an innie (ingoing) or outie (outgoing) has the most valid statistical correlation of all personality aspects studied, such as thinking and feeling (Johnson, Wiebe, and Gold 1999). As we mentioned earlier, these terms were created and popularized by Carl Jung. He was interested in people's patterns and tried to understand the vast differences between the viewpoints and approaches of his two colleagues Sigmund Freud and Alfred Adler, in order to relate to those "outside the clan." He noticed that Freud focused on adjusting to the outside world, so he used the term "extrovert" for him. Adler focused on the importance of the internal world, so he used the term "introvert" for him. Jung decided that the difference in their perceptions lay in each man's basic temperament and orientation. He thought both temperaments were useful and healthy.

Later, Adler and Jung had a falling out with Freud (as almost everyone who worked with Freud eventually did) over differing theoretical views. Freud was disappointed with Jung because he had expected him to be his successor and promote Freud's theories. Jung, however, had developed his own theories. Knowing Adler and Jung were both introverts, Freud, being angry at both of them, from that time forward wrote about introversion in a negative light. He described introverts as neurotic and self-absorbed, and he portrayed only extroverts as healthy. From this all-too-human conflict emerged the roots of the negative view of introverts and positive view of extroverts that, unfortunately, still holds true today.

Adaptable Temperaments

Like the ancient philosophers, modern scientists studying temperament find that almost all species can be divided into two groups: the hesitant and the bold. They think that this pattern has survived over millions of years of evolution because it makes us more adaptable to our changing environments. For instance, researchers (Zimmer 2005) have found that when food is scarce hesitant birds fit the environment better, since they fight less, eat less, and reproduce less. Bold birds don't fare as well. When food is plentiful, bold birds do better, because they fight more, eat more, and reproduce faster. Hesitant birds can't compete with so much aggression, so they don't do as well. Both temperaments contribute to the survival of the species by adapting to changing environments.

French journalist Alexis de Tocqueville (1969), an astute observer of human nature, wrote in *Democracy in America* about his nine-month tour of the United States in 1831. Noticing the abilities of both bold and hesitant Americans, he said that our budding country was initially populated and developed by indispensable people who speak out and take action. However, he cautioned Americans that, although these qualities would be useful in a new country, our society's long-term survival would depend upon maintaining a balance between active go-getters and quiet, reflective people who pause and think before acting.

America has ignored the red flags de Tocqueville waved. We continue to see extroverts as the ideal (Whybrow 2005). Yet society can't grow in a sustainable way without the balance introverts offer. Unfortunately, most innies feel overlooked, undervalued, and misunderstood, which keeps them from knowing their own gifts and showing them to the world. Our cultural tendency to judge temperaments as good or bad also filters down into individual relationships (Golden 1994). We forget that both temperaments have relational and cultural value that increases our chances of survival in our constantly changing environment.

Know Yourself and Your Partner

You can never learn too much about yourself or your partner. Knowing your and your partner's gifts and limitations builds relationship muscles. However, assessing temperament isn't always as easy as it sounds. Temperaments can be confusing because they are influenced by rising and falling energy levels. A person's environment can also influence whether he or she appears more introverted or more extroverted at any given time. And, in a similar vein, some innies have learned to pass as extroverts because of the intense pressure to be outgoing. So, the more you know about your partner's tendencies, preferences, and thought processes, the better you'll understand his or her temperament.

Couple Pillars

Some people rush out to meet life; others peek at it from around the corner before deciding when to venture out. Just this one aspect of temperament can affect your relationships in profound ways. Knowing your own temperament helps you identify your inborn talents, basic needs, core values, and chief motivations. It helps you know whether you are hesitant or bold, and what fills and drains your energy tank. Knowing yourself better increases your ability to recognize similarities and differences between you and your partner. With this knowledge, you can create the central pillars needed for a healthy relationship.

Couples require five strong pillars to establish and sustain love and connection in a relationship—and to support the relationship's structure. The first pillar, as we have discussed, is an effort by both partners to know themselves. The second pillar is a commitment to personally develop and grow. The third pillar is a solid understanding of the importance of give and take. The fourth pillar is the use of communication and negotiation skills to achieve cooperation. And the fifth pillar is acceptance, which allows partners to appreciate and adapt to one another.

How to Spot an Innie or Outie

Look over the lists of innie and outie tendencies below. Which profile do you fit better? Which does your partner fit? Ask each other what you think about yourself and your partner. Discuss differing opinions. If you're somewhere in the middle and can't tell which way you lean, think about what you need most: innies need more quiet time and outies require more outside stimulation. Or you can go to our Web site (www .hiddengifts.net) and complete the thirty-question "Introvert/Extrovert Questionnaire."

Innies may have the following tendencies

- They think before they act or speak.
- They make good eye contact when listening, less so when speaking.
- When speaking they have soft voices, appear calm, pause frequently, may sound hesitant, and may hunt for words.
- They enjoy solitude and feel drained after too much socializing.
- They prefer one-on-one conversing to party patter.
- They have one or two good friends.

Outies may have the following tendencies

- They shoot from the hip and the lip.
- They act first and think later.
- They have good eye contact when speaking, less so when listening.
- When speaking they show facial expressions, move their body, interrupt others, speak loudly, sound authoritative, and have a silver tongue.
- They enjoy excitement, plenty of activities, and socializing and feel drained by too much solitude.
- They consider lots of folks to be their friends.
- They love party chatter.

Set Points

As shown in the illustration below, the innie-outie continuum extends between two poles: extreme introversion and extreme extroversion.

E _____ I

We are all born with our personal "set points" (where we function best) located somewhere between those two poles (Bloom, Beal, and Kupper 2003). Of course, we all must use both sides of the continuum. But we also have one side that is dominant. Based on our genetics, each of us will tend toward either the innie or the outie side of the continuum, rather like we do with right- or left-handedness. We function best if we stay within our comfort zone, the area surrounding our set point. The continuum allows humans to be flexible. We can function outside of our comfort zone for a time, but then our bodies and brains become stressed. When stressed, our energy is drained and we don't function well. If stress goes on too long our health and performance can be damaged. For this and many other reasons, then, it's highly important that we each know our own temperament and set point (as well as our partner's). That way, we can keep our batteries charged, stay in our comfort zone most of the time, and keep stress to a minimum.

So what's your set point? Estimate where yours is located. Once you've read the book, come back to this page and see if you still agree with your initial estimate. You may find that you need to adjust your estimation of your set point based on what you've learned.

Fresh Footwork

Couples develop ingrained relational dance steps based on each partner's temperament. After a while, you may find yourself on automatic pilot when you execute your dance. You only know how to cha-cha, for example. You cha-cha forward, and he cha-chas back; he gets mad and you stomp out; and so on. It's hard to change these ingrained patterns. But you can do it. Armed with your new knowledge of temperament, you and your partner can attempt some newfangled footwork. When you know each other better, you can team up, try new steps, and create fresh combinations. You can even have some fun. You may step on each other's toes a few times, but just keep practicing. Learning new ways of relating to each other improves trust and flexibility, reduces conflict and stress, and increases your ability to resolve conflicts. Have a good time fox-trotting through the chapters ahead. ♡

2

all brains aren't the same

innie and outie hardwiring

"To understand the brain it is important to grasp
that it is the end product of a long process of evolution."
—Francis Crick

If you are an innie, you may wonder why your extroverted partner turns into a Chatty Cathy doll, complete with rosy face and shining eyes, after a party. If you are an outie you may wonder why you had to drag your innie partner out of the house, kicking and screaming, to that very same party. The answer? Your brains aren't the same.

Some years back, John Gray's *Men Are from Mars, Women Are from Venus* (1993) became a runaway best seller. Why did it hit such a nerve? We think it was because Gray described behaviors we were all beginning to notice about males and females. Although Gray used stereotypes in his books, they rang a bell with millions of couples. For example, most women were familiar with the typical guy behavior that sends him racing away to the garage to catch a little "cave time" (in other words, time alone to process emotions). Let's understand why and how this happens.

Male-Female Brain Differences

Today, neuroscientists use brain scans to pinpoint the areas that differ in men and women. For instance, women have a larger communication bridge connecting the right and left brain hemispheres (Hines 2004). It enables gals to have more crosstalk between the two hemispheres. Evolutionary psychologists think that women, because they may become moms, need to be brain ambidextrous. Childrearing requires combining the right hemisphere's emotional capacity with the left side's logical skills. Women need to shift smoothly from using just one side to using both sides simultaneously. Men have a smaller bridge so they don't coordinate both sides as easily. Therefore, they need that cave time so they can integrate emotions and reason.

Gender is only one way that the brain influences relationships. Another vital influence is temperament. In fact, temperaments may influence relationships even more than gender. In this chapter we will explore how differences in the brain can determine a person's temperament.

We will explain how the introvert's front brain functioning and the extrovert's back brain processing produce different behavior patterns. We will also touch on the right and left brain hemispheres' different strengths. Although humans are unpredictable at times, neuroscience can explain our universal behavior patterns. When you understand basic innie and outie qualities and behaviors, you will be better able to appreciate your partner without getting quite so frustrated.

Gray Matters

How do the three pounds of tiny gray cells perched inside your skull influence your temperament? To find out, first we'll need to understand at least a bit about our incredible, pinkish gray brain. Woody Allen alluded to how fascinating the brain is when he said, "The brain is my second favorite organ." The brain is so important that one-half of our genes are dedicated to hatching it. Yet when we are born it is not yet fully developed and requires years to mature. As Dr. Stephen Hinshaw states, "We know that the frontal lobes, which manage both feeling and thinking, don't mature fully until age thirty" (Kluger 2003).

So we begin with a half-baked noodle. We are born with some prewired brain cells so that we enter the world with basic survival skills— for example, once we develop some mobility, we can flee automatically or withdraw when we sense danger. But the rest of the brain is filled with millions of isolated brain cells (neurons) that must be linked together in order to develop our brain power. It's an amazing process, shaped by each person's genetic endowment and life experiences. If all goes well, by our late twenties some neurons have been strung into pathways, and unused cells are sloughed off. Now we have a fully baked noodle.

But what do all those little brain cells do anyway? Your brain's primary assignment is to keep you alive. To remain alive, we need to be able to make sense of ourselves and the world around us. This is no mean trick. The brain is bombarded with huge amounts of data coming from our inside and outside worlds. Somehow it must adjust to new input while preserving equilibrium. In this way, the brain is similar to an orchestra conductor, who coordinates each instrument into a harmonious symphony. The brain, like the conductor, selects, decreases, increases, blends, ignores, and balances individual opposing elements to make music. But the brain's mission is even more challenging than that of the conductor: it must do the equivalent of composing the music while conducting *and* giving a performance.

Maintaining balance is a constant challenge for the mind and body. The brain stores old perceptions, assimilates new data, and, like a television news station, informs the body of changes, or "breaking news." The brain says, "This just in! Your temperature is dropping. You are getting cold. Put on a coat, do some jumping jacks, turn up the heat, or start shaking to raise your body temperature." Your brain runs through the options and chooses the best survival tactic. "Do I have time to warm up by jacking up the heat? Should I do something quicker like tackling a few jumping jacks?" The brain struggles to maintain a stable environment by continually picking from among thousands of opposing alternatives, such as action or inaction, thinking or feeling, sleeping or waking, being or doing, speed or accuracy, and focusing internally or focusing externally. This last balancing act, interior versus exterior, is one of our most difficult balances to achieve. We need both to live: these two complex hard-wired systems (temperaments) help us maintain awareness of both what's happening inside and what's up outside (Solms and Turnbull 2002).

In everyday circumstances the brain is constantly attending and burning gallons of fuel in an effort to maintain balance between all of the alternatives. Twenty-four hours a day it is guessing, selecting, adjusting, and evaluating responses. It's a full-time job. That's why your brain may feel, at times, like a limp noodle. When it's been working hard for long periods, it may not always have the necessary awareness and high-octane fuel to respond to emergencies. Temperament makes the brain's job easier because it provides automatic responses to basic situations. It reduces the brain's need for attention and extra emergency fuel. In emergencies, introverts' automatic response is usually to pause and think before they act, and they may or may not decide to take action. In the same situation, extroverts will generally act first and think later. With these predetermined responses in place, the brain is able to conserve energy and continue composing, conducting, and performing throughout the day.

Stacked Deck

The brain's hierarchical design offers us incredible flexibility (Ratey 2002). Five levels are figuratively stacked on top of each other like the parts of a hamburger. Each level has evolved over millions of years of adaptation as more sophisticated abilities were built on top of primitive reactions. Many thousands of years ago, on the sweltering savanna, humans functioned from the bottom of the brain; they had the basic skills necessary to hunt, eat, and mate. Eventually, evolution added layers to the brain enabling humans to utilize complex skills, like caring for others outside our clan, self-reflection, and self-awareness. These abilities increased our survival rate by allowing us to override our primitive behaviors when necessary. The top of the brain now offers us an array of innovative and complex responses.

Our stacked deck increases our brain power because it provides us with the ability to respond to the environment in both simple and complex ways. Each level of the brain has parallel pathways integrating information at intersecting junctions (called association areas). These pathway options allow us to adapt and choose lower-level, simple responses or higher-level, complex responses as needed. This way, lower, unconscious, simple, and quick reactions are duplicated at higher, more sophisticated levels. Think back to a time when a driver cut you off and you automatically experienced a flash of anger because you felt threatened. Perhaps another time, when a driver suddenly cut in front of you, you felt fear but you also remembered you were okay. In that situation, your higher brain reminded you that you weren't in danger, so your anger didn't flash. Snap judgments are triggered by immediate, lower-level reactions, as illustrated in the first scenario. Well-planned, resourceful responses, like the reaction in the second scenario, are initiated in higher brain stacks. But it takes time to integrate information from various pathways.

One fact about the brain may surprise you: most levels operate outside of our awareness. Although it's a myth that we use only about 10 percent of our brain power, it is a fact that little brain functioning is conscious. Can you imagine being aware of all the adjustments your body is making every single minute? A little voice would be saying, "Lift your heel, shift your balance a bit to the right, dilate your pupils, increase your blood pressure, release some stomach acid, look to the left . . ." It would be impossible to get anything done. Fortunately, we don't need to be conscious of these automatic functions, but we do need to increase our awareness of our thoughts and feelings. And it takes effort and practice to become aware of the reactions driving our behavior. Knowing ourselves, our temperament, and our thoughts and feelings can guide our choices.

MAPPING THE BRAIN

In the last decade science has expanded our knowledge of the brain by leaps and bounds. We still have lots to learn but we are now much clearer about what's happening in our stacked deck. Using brain scans scientists can observe the pathways, junctions, and networks that organize the brain. While lying down in a scanning machine, patients are asked to speak or think about a particular topic. Their brain activity is observable because brain regions that are active and using energy light up on the scans. By tracking the activity in the brain, researchers map the various regions of the brain and give each an "address." Scientists have learned that each area of the brain is highly specialized and responsible for a particular function. If a particular brain address is active, we now know what the corresponding behaviors or activities will be. And even more amazing is the fact that the brain can use multiple sections together for complex functioning.

In order to study the relationship between the brain and behaviors, scientists slice and dice the brain in several ways. Dividing it into five (formerly thought to be four) lobes is the most common. Each lobe has its own duty. The occipital lobe processes vision. The parietal lobe processes sensory data from the body. The temporal lobe processes auditory information, like music and language. The frontal lobe processes two types of movement: thinking (considered to be movement in the brain) and the voluntary movement of muscles. This lobe is the CEO of complex functioning, such as speaking, emotional intelligence, decision making, reasoning, remembering, self-control, problem solving, and planning. The fifth lobe, the insula, has recently received a lot of attention from scientists because it appears to control many of our higher functions by integrating input from the other four lobes.

Another way scientists divide the brain is right down the middle. As we mentioned earlier, the brain is separated into right and left hemispheres, with a bridge connecting the two halves. Evolutionary psychologists think each side is specialized so we can use our hands independently. For example, one hand holds the baby while the other hand stirs the pot. (Nature may have goofed here, though, because any mother knows we really need three hands.) For more discrete and complex tasks, both hands and hemispheres must work together. The right brain controls the less action-oriented left side of the body and regulates emotions, intuition, and artistic abilities. The left brain shines when performing cognitive, language, and math skills and controls the more action-oriented right side of the body. The right brain creates a melody, for example, while the left brain (generally using the right hand) jots it down. We will discuss how each hemisphere affects relationships later in the chapter.

The last brain divide we will mention is the separation at the central sulcus between the front and the back of the brain. Debra Johnson, John Wiebe, and Sherri Gold (1999) reported a PET scan study showing that introverts use the front of the brain and extroverts use the back of the brain (see illustration on page 44). The back of the brain, where extroverts hang out, is considered the "being" part of the brain (the part of the brain used for reacting in the moment). When the back part of the brain is used, sensory data creates a candid snapshot of a perception, which activates basic behaviors. It's similar to what happens when you run a red light: as you zoom through the intersection, the police camera automatically snaps a photo of your speeding car and you receive a ticket in the mail. The front of the brain, where introverts spend more of their time, is the "doing" part of the brain (the part used for reflecting before acting). In this area, sensory data, old and new memories, thinking, and feeling contribute to the development of a *National Geographic*–quality photo. Here the shot is researched, planned, traveled to, and tested until a particular photo is created. Based on these fleshed-out perceptions, complex thinking and intentional behaviors are selected and initiated.

THE FIVE STACKS

Let's tour the decks and see what each does. Later in the chapter, when we explain the innie and outie mind-and-body systems, you may want to refer back to this section.

The First Stack: Lizard Brain

The brain stem is our lizard brain, which developed more than 280 million years ago. It is the first level that registers sensory input; it doesn't think or learn but simply maintains and regulates unconscious survival functions: feeding, fleeing, fighting, and reproduction. Cold-blooded, aggressive, predatory behaviors are created here.

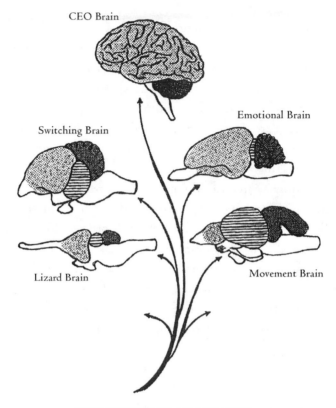

CEO Brain

Emotional Brain

Switching Brain

Lizard Brain

Movement Brain

THE WHOLE BRAIN STACKS

The Second Stack: Movement Brain

The cerebellum, which evolved next, coordinates skilled repetitive movements and fluid motions, balance, and posture. This layer is the foundation for many higher relationship functions. For instance, it establishes the crucial ability to take turns, or go back and forth with others—the basis for dancing, talking, and sharing. (Since the two of us met in a college dance class, we consider it a good thing that we both function smoothly in this area.)

The Third Stack: Emotional Brain

The limbic system, our emotional region, evolved after the cerebellum. It allows humans to take a huge step forward beyond unthinking lizard living. All incoming sensations (except smell) travel to the limbic area to be processed. This area influences mood and houses the emotional threat system. Pain, fear, and anger are triggered when real or imagined threats are perceived. Smells take a shorter route and they are quickly registered here—so we can sniff out danger. Scents also enhance pleasures like eating and sex.

This emotional area fuels motivation, stores and selects memories, and guides our emotional interactions with others. This is a key area, which allows us to work and play well with others. Without this layer of the brain your partner would be like a snake or a lizard—he or she wouldn't even know your name. Emotions are the foundation for the development of empathy and connections and they alert us to changes that are needed in the relationship. Paying attention to your emotional signals can improve your relationship and strengthen your connections with the ones you love.

The Fourth Stack: Switching Brain

The hypothalamus and thalamus function to sift and sort incoming stimuli (except smells). The hypothalamus evaluates the constant input and accordingly adjusts functions like hormone levels, temperature, adrenal output, sleeping, drinking, and eating. Depending on what is needed it activates either the "spending" or "conserving" side of the autonomic nervous system (we'll talk more about this important system later on). The thalamus selects vital input from the sensory, visual, and auditory systems and amplifies or decreases it, shuttling it onto higher integration areas.

The Fifth Stack: CEO Brain

This brain region, which allows us to execute sophisticated and complex functions, is the new kid on the block. It developed only 80 million years ago. Perceptions are developed from reflecting on thoughts, feelings, past and future experiences, and mixed emotions. Plans are created and evaluated as a result of these perceptions, and choices are made. Thoughts, ideas, starting actions, stopping actions, and speaking are produced here. This area overrides lower brain levels with the crucial ability to say no to ourselves.

This layer of the brain is humanity central. It gives us the ability to develop trust, feel empathy, share ourselves, develop self-awareness, put others' needs first, make mutual decisions, and set goals. It allows us to establish, repair, grow, and maintain a satisfying relationship, and it gives us the ability to know we have a "self." It is this self-knowledge and capacity for self-control that sets us apart from other animals on the planet.

Home on the Temperament Range

Despite having the same basic brain structure, each of us has genes that whip up chemicals designed to make a one-of-a-kind brain. What makes humans both unique and similar? According to Stephen Gould in *The Mismeasure of Man*, "Genes set limits to ranges, they do not provide blueprints for an exact replica" (1996, 359).

Our parents pass down their genes, which contain recipes to create our neurotransmitters. "Considerable evidence has been amassed to support the view that some traits, such as the extent to which one is extroverted or introverted, are highly influenced by one's genetic history," says leading neuroscientist Joseph LeDoux in *Synaptic Self* (2003, 29). How does this occur? Like ice cream, neurotransmitters come in a wide variety of flavors. Our genetic recipes make different amounts of each flavor. Every flavor creates a separate pathway through the brain switching on or off specialized functions. Introverts' genes produce more of the neurotransmitter "flavor" acetylcholine (Pepeu 2004), which activates conscious movement of the body, selects or "tags" memories to be stored in long-term memory, initiates REM sleep, triggers consciousness and concentration, and runs the parasympathetic conserving side of the nervous system (Lester and Berry 1998). Extroverts' genes make more of one flavor of dopamine (there are five flavors) (Rammsayer 1998). Dopamine is a major reward neurotransmitter that is involved in feeling excited, unconsciously moving the body, and triggering the sympathetic spending side of the nervous system (Stelmack 1990).

HOW DOPAMINE & ACETYLCHOLINE FUNCTION

In order to better understand how our brains work, let's take a look at their hankering for a neurotransmitter like dopamine or acetylcholine (depending on whether we're an outie or an innie). We'll first track the activity that occurs when dopamine is released in response to input to the back of the brain. Clusters of cells that like its flavor lick it up and "fire," or turn on. When clusters of these cells fire at the same time, they wire together, creating pathways (Swickert and Gilliland 1998). The more the neurotransmitter flows down the pathway, the more established it becomes. Extroverted qualities and behaviors are initiated as dopamine travels its short pathway. Unused neurons are sloughed off, streamlining and increasing the brain's performance. Well-used pathways develop grooves so that the cells can fire even faster. Similarly, acetylcholine is released in the front of the brain and, unlike dopamine, travels a longer, more complex pathway. Temperaments are just grooved pathways triggering the same behavior patterns. Grooves can also become ruts that we call habits—and that is why habits are so hard to break.

Innie & Outie Hardwiring

Marti began to search for the physiological underpinnings of both introverted and extroverted temperaments because she had noticed such incredible differences between Mike and herself. In this section we will explain how innie and outie hardwiring creates so many opposing qualities and behaviors. Main pathways travel through five layers of the brain, connecting functions on all levels. The innie's complex pathway travels up to the front of the brain, and the outie's direct pathway travels to the back of the brain.

We are all born with two basic mental energy systems. The introverted system restores the mind and body, generating energy by relaxing, attending to ideas, planning, imagining, meditating, thinking, and feeling. The extroverted system energizes the mind and body by initiating stimulating experiences with people, things, and activities. All of us need to use both systems, but we function best in life if we are in our comfort zone, around our set point, most of the time. First, we will take a spin around the outie system. Then we'll do a lap around the innie system. Enjoy the journey!

LET'S TRAVEL THE OUTIE SYSTEM

The extroverted brain has lower blood flow and lower internal activity than the introvert's brain. It scans the environment in order to collect stimuli to trigger dopamine, which in turn activates the most exciting reward pathway. This shorter pathway turns on the body's spending fight, flight, or fright side of the autonomic nervous system. Working in conjunction, the dopamine brain pathway and the spending side of the nervous system create the abilities, qualities, and behaviors we observe in extroverts. If claimed, tamed, and aimed, this system can accomplish quite a lot.

Dr. Johnson's study, mentioned earlier, used PET scans to map the brain locations (addresses) where introverts and extroverts showed brain activity. In Marti's original research, she took the addresses that Dr. Johnson had sited and found that each followed a specific neurotransmitter pathway. Innies' addresses were on the acetylcholine pathway and outies' were located on a dopamine pathway. She also found that each pathway activated different sides of the nervous system. Since then, other studies have validated Dr. Laney's hypothesis that extroverts' brain activity relies upon a dopamine pathway and switches on the spending side of the nervous system. Now we are going to travel that pathway, stopping to check out what each location does.

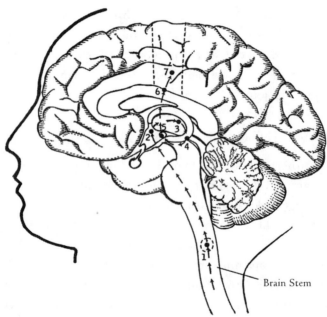

SHORTER EXTROVERT DOPAMINE PATHWAY

1. Reticular Activating System (RAS)

Located in the brain stem just above the spine, the RAS collects sensory input and intensifies it. Dopamine is released. It activates a jolt of great-feeling "hap hits" (what researchers call a "good feeling of happiness") (Howard 2001). The back attention system (BAS) is activated in the rear of the brain to focus on any movement that catches the eye. This is why Mike enjoys state fairs, crowded stores, and scouting any environment for hap hits. Movement, or the anticipation of something new and exciting, grabs his interest and increases his excitement.

2. Hypothalamus

The hypothalamus regulates the most basic body functions, such as thirst, temperature, and appetite. New input is mixed with old memories and other data in the parietal lobe of the brain to create snap perceptions. This quick-acting system is great for action and emergencies but it can create impulsiveness. It craves stimuli and attention. This makes it difficult for outies to rest and relax. These snap perceptions turn on the spending side of the autonomic nervous system (see illustration on page 40). It prepares the body for high-energy action: fighting, fleeing, or doing. Pupils dilate to improve vision. Blood pressure and pulse are increased to help get the body moving. Oxygen in the lungs is increased to facilitate movement. Adrenaline, norepinephrine, and glucose surge to the torso in order to gear up for action. Internal duties, such as metabolizing food and excretion, are shut down. Mike enjoys the feeling of energy and aliveness when this system is engaged. He can go without food or sleep for long periods. He moves without thinking. He thrives on stress, excitement, and emergencies, and he responds to these by taking action. Exercise feels invigorating. Energy is created when stimuli or stress releases the powerhouses of dopamine, adrenaline, norepinephrine, glucose, and oxygen. Lively, fast-paced chatting, with lots of eye contact, fuels this system. Listening doesn't. When he's alone, quiet, or reflecting, using the conserving side of the nervous system, only acetylcholine is released. Acetylcholine hap hits (Howard 2001) are barely noticeable to him because they aren't intense enough. He feels drained and loses energy if he goes very long without jolts from his high-octane fuel system.

3. Thalamus

The thalamus is a relay station. Sensory input is amplified and relayed to association areas higher up in the brain.

4. Amygdala

The amygdala is the emotional center, where fear, anxiety, pain, and anger are triggered to respond to a real or perceived threat. Dopamine is released in reaction to threats. Preprogrammed reactions are triggered without the involvement of higher thinking. Mike, like most outies, reacts automatically to intense emotions and becomes irritated easily because of this quick-draw threat system. This system allows him to respond quickly to a threat or danger, but it is likely to be triggered by someone who is different—which may explain why outies generally like other outies and find innies annoying.

5. Back Insula

The insula is now considered the fifth lobe of the brain. Here, input from pathways in the other four lobes (frontal, temporal, occipital, and parietal) are integrated. Two sensory pathways, which form an essential part of the brain's alert system, are combined and processed in the insula. These two pathways, the conscious, fast-acting vision pathway and the speedy auditory pathway, help us locate possible threats, objects, or people we are seeking.

The alert system makes snap judgments based on a smell, noise, or shadow and tells the person to take action. Together with the action side of Mike's nervous system, the alert system provides quick responses to sensory data from the outside world. This is how a family member can be mistaken for an intruder, for example. When Mike hears an unfamiliar sound at night, he might look at Marti with a quizzical expression and quickly hop out of bed to investigate.

6. Cingulate Gyrus

The cingulate is a vital intersection between brain regions. The cingulate has two paths that can be chosen. Extroverts take the cingulated gyrus fork, activating a variety of party skills. Emotions loosen the tongue, and, like the lower-level switch in the hypothalamus, they switch on the flight, fight, or fright system from this location. Dopamine releases hap hits and heightens attention to the outside world. This back attention system scans the environment, trolling for quick-paced stimuli like cocktail-party patter. This explains Mike's enjoyment of social chit-chat and his desire to prolong parties. It also accounts for his love of variety and new experiences and is the reason he needs to have the TV off when concentrating and sleeping.

The other fork in this pathway travels through the left mid-cingulate, called the "social secretary to the CEO" in the frontal lobes. Extroverts gain entry to this area when they can stop and shut out external stimuli to focus inward. Now, Mike can concentrate and reflect to construct complex perceptions. When he slows down and concentrates, he enters this area, where planning, analytical thinking, and evaluating occur. If outies stay in this innie-preferred area for a lengthy period, however, they usually get antsy.

7. Temporal Lobe

This seventh and last stop is where sensory information, learning, and emotions are integrated and processed. Alpha brain waves are activated here reflecting an alert state. Short-term memory operates here. This is an outie's strong suit—just don't ask an outie later what he or she learned a week ago. It may not have been stored in long-term memory, so now it's gone. However, outies' short-term memory helps them perform well under pressure, such as when they're cramming for a test or spitting out a snappy comeback. This area integrates input, decides on conscious actions, and signals the motor area to move body muscles. Because of their strong short-term memory and ability to perform under pressure, extroverts like Mike are comfortable when they have deadlines, exams, and presentations. And, as a result, outies tend to do well in our school systems and work environments. However, not remembering what their partner said to them last week can be a relational problem. Plus, in the absence of pressure outies may sometimes have trouble motivating themselves.

LET'S TRAVEL THE INNIE SYSTEM

The introverted brain has more blood flow and higher internal activity than that of an extrovert, so it is constantly cogitating. While brain activity in an introvert is heightened, the person's inhibitory system "tunes out" the environment, reducing external stimuli and dopamine jolts. Acetylcholine is one of the most influential neurotransmitters in the brain so it affects innies in many ways. Internal thought, speech, concentration, intimate conversations, and personal interests are "bathed" by acetylcholine. When the interesting or personal experience gets its acetylcholine dip it is tagged as important and stored into long-term memory. Innies also receive mild hap hits from acetylcholine. In addition, acetylcholine fuels the conserving side of the nervous system.

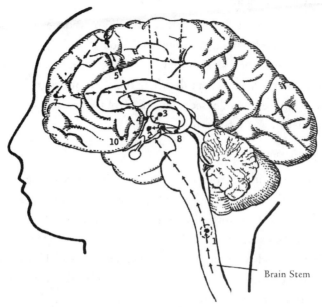

Brain Stem

LONGER INTROVERT ACETYLCHOLINE PATHWAY

The combination creates the abilities, qualities, and behaviors we notice in introverted people. Their pathway is longer, collects more details, and gathers more unconscious input, so it takes more time to process information. Innies also need to sleep after receiving input, since information and experiences are stored into long-term memory during sleep.

Introverts have memories like elephants; the trick is to know how to retrieve those memories. They are retrieved in two ways. One way is through sensory information, like the aroma of your grandmother's kitchen or the sight of a photograph that reminds you of your childhood. The second way is through association, in which the person allows his or her mind to hop from thought to thought, associating or linking together old memories. Because of these processes, innies' memories take time to snag.

1. Reticular Activating System (RAS)

In an innie brain, this area receives stimuli and reduces it—the opposite of what an outie brain does. Innies may look glazed if they are flooded with input, because they already have very active brains. In fact, innies often look away to reduce stimuli when they are hunting for words or talking. Acetylcholine is released when the front attention system (FAS) signals, "Something is interesting."

2. Hypothalamus

As is the case with extroverts, the hypothalamus regulates basic body functions like thirst, temperature, and appetite. But, unlike the extrovert's hypothalamus, the introvert's hypothalamus turns on the "conserving" side of the nervous system. (See illustration on page 40.) It is responsible for repairing the body and recharging and storing energy. Unlike the outie system, which runs on various types of fuel, the innie system runs only on acetylcholine. When it is released, the introvert's pupils contract and reduce incoming light; saliva increases; food is metabolized; mating can occur; muscles move if consciously instructed; and breathing, blood pressure, and pulse all decrease. Marti, like most innies, appears calm, speaks in a soft voice, pauses between words, doesn't move her face or body much, can sit for hours, doesn't enjoy exercise, moves slowly, and needs to eat often to keep her glucose levels up. Her feet and hands get hot and cold easily. Yet, she can still be observant and very alert while attending to someone or something. Anything that requires energy, like being in the outside world, having people in her space, dealing with conflict, and interacting with others, requires energy output and so is draining. She likes the familiar (since these situations burn less energy), needs to ease into new situations, and may not be able to think or make decisions around too much stimuli or too many people. If Mike's outie spending side is triggered, Marti may feel overstimulated and anxious. That outie dopamine jolt feels like drinking a gallon of black coffee to her.

3. Front Thalamus

This relay area receives external stimuli, reduces it, and shuttles it up to the frontal lobe, where the CEO of the brain is located.

4. Front Insular Lobe

This insular lobe is where input from the hearing, seeing, sensing, and CEO lobes are integrated. This area is called the "great inhibitor" —where actions can be stopped. This is why innies can say no to themselves. This area also accesses emotional intelligence, where complex emotional capacities such as empathy and self-reflection happen and emotional meanings are assigned. It can allow the person to hold complex thoughts in mind while making decisions. The slower and unconscious visual pathway identifies what objects, people, and behaviors are seen. It is slower because it picks up conscious and unconscious observations. The auditory pathway takes in more complex and unconscious information, so it requires more processing time. In addition, this area processes a number of slower complex pathways, so innies need more time before responding. This makes it hard for innies to give quick responses.

Innies, like Marti, have many strengths derived from this area of the brain. If they realize that they need time to be aware of all of this input they have valuable advantages. They are very observant when they are focusing on the world. However, since they are easily flooded they can appear somewhat distant. Marti uses her ability to self-reflect and empathize in her profession and relationships. She can quickly put herself in other people's shoes. Marti, like other innies, can delay gratification but sometimes she waits so long that she misses out on something. She reflects on complex concepts but she can noodle so much she doesn't take action. She needs to remind herself that she requires more time to integrate data than outies do before making decisions.

THE ACTIONS OF THE AUTONOMIC NERVOUS SYSTEM

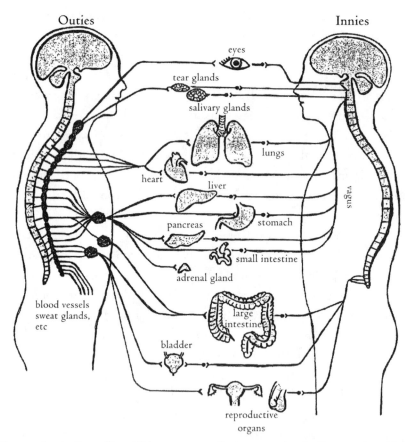

Outies

Innies

eyes
tear glands
salivary glands
lungs
heart
liver
pancreas
stomach
small intestine
adrenal gland
blood vessels sweat glands, etc
large intestine
bladder
reproductive organs
vagus

Sympathetic Spending Side
- Dilates pupils
- Decreases saliva
- Increases oxygen, heart rate, glucose, and adrenaline
- Decreases gastric juices
- Relaxes bladder
- Contracts rectum

Parasympathetic Conserving Side
- Contracts pupils
- Increases saliva
- Reduces oxygen, heart rate, glucose, and adrenaline
- Increases gastric juices
- Speeds up digestion
- Contracts bladder

5. Left Mid-Cingulate

The mid-cingulate is the social secretary to the frontal lobes (see number 6 on the outie pathway, shown in illustration on page 32). It grants entry into the CEO region. Based on emotions, this area prioritizes, directs attention, turns speaking on and off, and inhibits movement. Also based on emotions, it switches on and off the conserving side of the nervous system. When an introvert is concentrating on something interesting, this area directs attention internally, and external distractions are turned off. An innie using this area may appear zoned out, even though her brain is actually very active, and she may sit for hours without moving her body. When Marti is concentrating deeply, she can have difficulty switching off her concentration, and she may have trouble refinding her place if disturbed. She receives hap hits from acetylcholine, so concentrating on introversion for fifteen years is fun for her.

6. Broca's Area

This area plans speech movements and it's the home of "internal talk." Innies have lots of chatter going on in their brain. If they don't have interests to feed this chatterbox it often fills the void with self-criticism. It's crucial for outies to understand that innies don't have a mute button to turn off this chatter. This area is so busy in innies that they may even have trouble retrieving words from other language areas when needing to speak out loud, especially when they are tired, overstimulated, or stressed. Marti tries to fool her brain when she goes to bed, turning its attention outward by reading or watching TV. This can cause some conflicts since Mike, an outie, needs to reduce stimuli in order to go to sleep.

7. Frontal Lobes

This area is the CEO of the brain. In this region acetylcholine stimulates beta waves, creating the highest alert brain waves. Abstract thinking and REM dreaming (when memories are integrated during sleep) are activated. Complex social information is processed in order to make complicated decisions. This region loves to learn information and make sense of it. It's the home of free will. Selecting, planning, and choosing actions—which could be either internal actions like thoughts, feelings, or ideas, or external actions like body movements—based on thinking and feeling happen here.

This area looks to the future, creates expectations, imagines what might happen, and rehearses possible scenarios. All of these thinking steps are taken without ever actually moving the body. If the decision is made to take action, the outcome is later evaluated. Marti, for example, can imagine something she is going to do. She already has the steps decided and the actions planned. She sometimes doesn't see the point of actually doing it, or she might think she has already executed her plans. However, if she doesn't carry out the plans, at least occasionally, she cannot learn from real-world feedback. After she takes actions she rewinds the events and evaluates them. In this way, she, like most innies, learns from her experiences and stores the knowledge in her long-term memory for future use.

8. Hippocampus

The hippocampus tags experiences when they are personal by "washing" them with acetylcholine. It also selects, consolidates, stores, and retrieves short-term memories that have been broken up and stored into long-term memory. This is why Marti takes things personally—her experiences are remembered as personal. This tendency to take things personally can irritate outies, who don't normally store their own experiences as personal. If something or someone is interesting to Marti she stores the information in her long-term memory and, like an elephant, she seldom forgets. However, she sometimes needs to remember the "hook" that would help her retrieve the memory.

9. Amygdala

This area is often called the threat system. It reacts to real or perceived threats with fear, anxiety, pain, or anger. The hearing pathway and the threat system notice negative experiences and store them in memory. The amygdala connects feelings and thoughts, but, since it is at the end of the pathway, innies usually take a while to become fully aware of their emotional reactions. (This helps explain why innies are often considered unemotional. It is just a physiological aspect of being an introvert.) As a result, conflicts can seem scary and overwhelming. Marti, like most innies, may avoid conflicts because she knows it takes a long time and lots of energy to process her reactions.

10. Front Temporal Lobe

This temporal lobe processes emotions, sensory input, and learning from negative experiences. Here, short-term memory is activated by dopamine, so it doesn't function quite as well for right-brained innies. Left-brained innies have more dopamine so their short-term memory usually functions better. Slow and more-unconscious auditory and visual pathways are integrated as they travel through this area. The downside of the slow auditory pathway is that it registers memories of pain and displeasure when it is washed with acetylcholine. It's why Marti and other innies tend to remember and sometimes avoid negative experiences. However, it is also the reason innies learn from their experiences. Marti plans her actions based on her past experiences and makes better decisions in the future.

This area also sends signals to the voluntary motor area to direct muscles to move. Marti, like all innies, has to consciously think to move her body. Many innies don't know that they need to tell themselves out loud to move. Unfortunately, they usually think they are lazy, unmotivated, or overtired.

The Whole Brain & Actions of the Autonomic Nervous System

Temperament explains behaviors originating from the front and the back of the brain (Sarter, Givens, and Bruno 2001). But there's a bit more to it. To round out our discussion of the brain's influence we will mention the contributions from the right and left hemispheres (illustration below).

We all need to use both sides of our brains together, but everybody is influenced by one hemisphere more than the other. It's easy to determine whether people have a dominant right or left brain (Springer and Deutsch 1998). Left-brained folks explain the world by developing reasons based on logic. Right-brained people understand the world by developing reasons based on emotions. Each hemisphere organizes the world from its own vantage point.

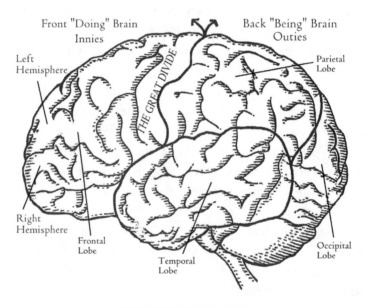

THE WHOLE BRAIN

Couples with thinking and feeling differences often clash over practical issues like values, needs, and wants. Discussions between a feeling (right-brained) partner and a thinking (left-brained) partner can be quite frustrating (we know this from personal experience). If left-brained Mike wants a new car he will show Marti the budget, with the expense and income columns all balanced and totaled. Then he will go over why buying a new car makes "perfect sense." He will expect Marti to see the beauty of his logic and agree. However, if she doesn't feel that we need or can afford a new car and is anxious about spending the money, then all the logic in the world will be meaningless to her. Mike might get annoyed because none of these reasons make sense to him, and Marti may feel that he doesn't care about her feelings. However, despite all of these differences, couples with different hemisphere contributions can make a good team. If they learn to listen to each other, by combining their thinking and feeling talents they can make better decisions.

Most people are left-brain dominant, and men tend to be more left-brain dominant than women. Some introverts are peppier than others, generally because they are left-brain dominant. Dopamine, the outie's favorite chemical flavor, is the main neurotransmitter for the left brain, so left-brained innies have more energy than their right-brained counterparts. Acetylcholine, the innie's favorite juice, is the main neurotransmitter for the right brain. Right-brained innies therefore can have even more trouble blasting their bodies off the sofa. In later chapters we will discuss several specific areas where right- and left-brain dominance affect relationships. You and your partner can look over the list below and see which one fits each of you better.

RELATIONAL CHARACTERISTICS OF RIGHT-BRAINERS

- Sees the forest rather than each tree
- Tolerates mixed feelings
- Is nonverbal, and more artistic
- Uses empathic and emotional language
- Emphasizes relationships
- Describes activities using metaphors and symbols
- Talks with others mainly to make connection
- Enjoys sharing personal experiences
- Asks questions about others' perspective and experiences
- Helps others come to their own decisions
- Changes mind if evidence suggests

RELATIONAL CHARACTERISTICS OF LEFT-BRAINERS

- Sees each redundant tree
- Uses black-and-white, right-and-wrong thinking
- Uses precise, logical, and authoritarian language
- Emphasizes independence and separation
- Communicates as a process of clarification
- Talks mainly in order to think things out
- Has an impersonal and objective style of speaking
- Asks questions to understand the others' logic
- Helps others find correct answer to their problems
- Makes evidence fit his or her opinion

LEFT AND RIGHT BRAIN FUNCTIONS

Left Brain

Controls the right side of the body

Understanding speech, reading, and speaking

Using language, writing

Understanding numbers, quantities, and calculations

Logical thinking-problem solving based on facts

Right Brain

Controls the left side of the body

Emotions, imagination, intuition, humor, and ideas

Expressive arts-playing music, painting, drawing, creative writing

Assessing perspective

Recognizing patterns, shapes, faces, and expressions

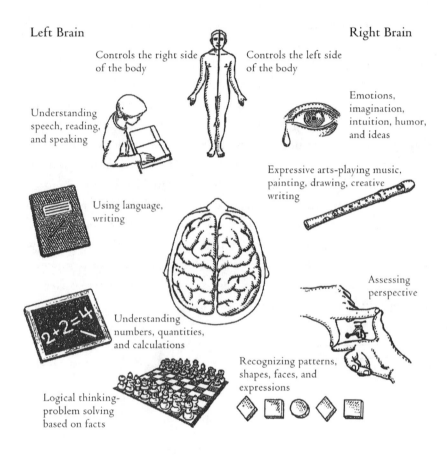

Strained Your Brain? --

If you have found this chapter confusing or overstimulating, we recommend that you reread it in small sections. You might want to discuss with your partner the various tendencies we've listed and how they apply to each of you. You can also use this chapter as a reference as you read the other chapters.

You and your partner exhibit behaviors that have become ingrained in humans over the course of millions of years of evolution. In general, your partner's irritating behaviors aren't personal, even if it seems like they are. Obviously, temperaments have a purpose or they would have disappeared long ago. However, it doesn't mean that we don't need to modify some of our behavior. Conflicts will be less heated between you and your partner when you remember that you are both acting in ways that have a purpose. Now that you understand the differences of your hardwired systems, you can appreciate and combine your strengths. Doing so will improve your relationship. Armed with this knowledge, you're now ready to explore how partners' temperament and brain-hemisphere differences influence different couple combinations. ♡

3

couple combinations

play the music and dance

"Maria, do you want to dance with me?"
—spoken by Ted Danson in the film <u>Cousins</u>
(screenplay by Stephen Metcalfe)

Every couple wants to swing and sway in unison to their own kind of music. But partners each enter the relationship with their own dance steps, learned while growing up in their family, community, and culture. Each partner's steps contain built-in biases and values—often without their even knowing they learned these steps. Without awareness we all think our own dance is the right one. "Doesn't everyone dance this way?" we say. Toes frequently get stepped on when the partners' unspoken patterns and expectations cause uncoordinated dance steps. But toe tromping can be avoided if the differences underlying and directing both partners' footwork are recognized and discussed.

Differences Make a Difference

The key word here is "differences"—which humans love to hate. Differences can either spice up or blow up your relationships. The first step to creating spicy yet flowing footwork together is to recognize your differences. We all enter into coupledom with individual differences that are based on many factors. Temperament is a big player, of course, but some of the other heavy hitters are age, gender, class, cultural or religious backgrounds, role expectations, and heart or head dominance. These individual traits and tendencies gradually become automatic steps. After a while, we are dancing with our partners as if we are on autopilot. By switching off your autopilot dancing and considering the origins of your steps, you'll increase your chances for a successful relationship. Now a new dance can be designed and choreographed to your own special couple music.

In this chapter we will explore several couple combos and their typical dance steps. First, we are going to discuss the dynamics of the most common pair, the waltzing female innie and male outie. The second couple, the tangoing innie male and outie female, has more challenges, since the partners are dancing to a tune that isn't the cultural norm. Third, we'll discuss the same-sex innie-outie couple, dancing the cha-cha, living with the constant awareness that they are out of step with our mainstream culture. Two other couple styles—the balletic innie-innie and the swinging outie-outie—will be briefly discussed. Exercises at the end of the chapter can help bring differences, values, and expectations in any partner combination to light. We also give suggestions about how to balance and strengthen your relationship, thereby increasing your appreciation and love.

IT HAPPENS TO ALL OF US

When Dr. Carlfred Broderick, head of the University of Southern California psychology department's Ph.D. program, gave a talk when Marti was in graduate school, he told a funny but valuable story that illustrated the dance steps we all learn from our original families. Dr. Broderick had been married for only a few months when he caught the flu bug. Like his family members did when they were sick, he went straight to bed and waited. And waited. And waited. But much to his surprise his lovely new wife didn't bring him the expected glass of orange juice. He wondered, Where is she? Doesn't she love me? Doesn't she care that I'm sick?

Meanwhile, his wife hummed "Whistle While You Work" as she tidied the apartment. She felt like a good wife. She waited for her groom to emerge from the bedroom signaling his recovery. She waited. And waited. Finally Dr. Broderick dragged his feverish body out of bed and snarled, "Where is my gosh darn orange juice?" She looked puzzled, but a few minutes later she arrived bearing a glass of juice. Later, when he was feeling better, they discussed what had happened. They learned that they had each grown up with different values about how to express love when someone is ill. In his family they valued waiting on the sick person, and love was shown by bringing the patient orange juice. (His family believed it was like a nectar from the gods that could cure any ailment.) In his bride's family they valued leaving the sick person alone to recover in peace. Supplying cave time meant they were showing love. Dr. Broderick and his wife laughed about the dance steps they had learned from their families. They went on to have a satisfying marriage, issuing a brood of eight children. They grew their own orange tree in their backyard.

Waltzing Traditional Couple: Introvert Female & Extrovert Male

The innie female and the outie male is the most traditional pairing. Jane Jones and Ruth Sherman write in their book, *Intimacy and Type*, "Our extensive clinical practice and research seems to indicate that the [introvert-extrovert] relationship works better if the male is the extrovert and the woman is the introvert" (1997, 106).

This type of pairing is still highly sanctioned by the culture and is often seen in political couples. Even the president and first lady, George and Laura Bush, admit that he's an outie and she's an innie. Other influences besides temperament are usually at work here as well, such as culture, role expectations, gender, and hemisphere dominance.

Traditional families were the topic of many 1950s TV shows, like the *Donna Reed Show*, *Father Knows Best*, *Ozzie and Harriet*, and many others. It is reflective of our changing culture that these couples aren't as prominent on TV or in films today. However, they still pop up now and then because they still exist. In the films *Father of the Bride I* and *II*, Steve Martin plays an outie father and Diane Keaton is cast as his innie wife. They live in the proverbial two-story colonial surrounded by a white picket fence. She calmly keeps their daughter's wedding plans on track while he runs his company and copes with losing his only daughter to marriage.

This couple combination functions very well especially if the partners are from cultures that expect the man to be in charge. They often have less conflict because their roles are well defined and sanctioned by the culture. When this couple is working well together they create a nourishing home base for their family balanced with activity in the outside world. We began our marriage with this traditional pattern. Mike came from a 1950s-sitcom-model family. Marti's folks had a nontraditional pattern, but her temperament and wish for stability were well suited for a traditional waltz.

In our first years of marriage, we followed the traditional pattern: Mike worked full-time and Marti stayed home raising our daughters. Women who are introverted are usually homebodies and enjoy creating a cozy nest. Though many innies don't have children, they can enjoy the pace of childrearing and homemaking if they have adequate recharging time and aren't too overwhelmed. When an innie is working outside the home (unless it's a solitary, quiet type of work), raising children and homemaking in addition to working can cause her to run out of steam fast. In this case, it will be important for the innie to ask for help. She will need her partner, relatives, or paid help to assist her in managing work, home, and children.

FAMILIARITY BREEDS CONNECTION

Intimacy is being familiar with another—connecting by talking about your innermost thoughts and feelings and listening to your partner's private thoughts and feelings. The traditional couple can run into intimacy problems, especially if the woman is a right-brained innie and the man is a left-brained outie. Although many writers say outies want too much conversation from their innie partner, it's actually a bit more complicated than that. An innie's openness to or need for conversation really depends on many factors. If the innie's job or children give her lots of close, personal interactions, she may not need more intimacy from her outie partner. In this case, the outie partner may interpret her lower need for intimacy as a personal rejection and feel ignored or undervalued. In the opposite case, when the innie's work and daily activities do not provide plenty of personal interaction, she will need more intimacy and personal conversations with her outie partner. But most outies prefer a style of relating that we might call "conversation lite." If an outie engages in nothing but snappy patter with his spouse, the innie may become frustrated because that interaction doesn't provide the complexity she needs to spark her interest and generate hap hits. On the other hand, if the outie exhausts his relating firepower at work, he may become pretty quiet at home. He may even take a dive or two into his cave. In this case the innie partner is left without a close person to share her inner life with.

So the irony here is that innies, contrary to popular opinion, actually need more intimacy while outies often don't. The right-brained innie female especially needs a deep connection with her partner. Establishing one or two close friendships is crucial for this innie if her partner isn't interested or cannot be intimate. Marti has counseled many female innies who enjoy psychotherapy because it gives them the recharging that comes from making a deeper emotional connection. It actually helps them stay married to their outie, who loves to chat about news, weather, and sports. If the outie talks his partner's arm and leg off about what she considers meaningless chatter, he may need to take that energy and find some pals who enjoy shooting the chatty breeze. As you can see, it's important to keep a dialogue going about how much and what type of interacting each of you wants or needs.

Since this pairing is still burned into our psyche as the Western cultural ideal, with the woman behind the man, the relationship usually goes well unless the innie partner wants to step out. In an interview in a documentary titled *Washington Wives*, author and Washington society maven Sally Quinn remarked that Americans weren't ready for the political wives we saw in the 2004 presidential election. Howard Dean's wife, Dr. Judith Dean, said she would keep practicing medicine if he got elected, and John Kerry's spouse, Teresa Heinz Kerry, received lots of flack for speaking her mind. Quinn said, "Americans still want traditional couples where the wife gazes up at her husband with adoration." But if a male outie *wants* a powerful wife who equals or outshines him, then the relationship isn't as threatened. In our interviews with this type of couple, they often described the strengths and stressors listed below.

When this couple's strengths are in tune:

- They don't compete for attention.
- Innie nurtures the relationship.
- Each offers balance to the other.
- Outie expands the innie's experiences in the world.
- Innie encourages outie to slow down and enjoy hearth and home.
- Innie keeps the outie focused.
- Outie can, at times, speak up for the innie.
- Outie has the limelight.

When this couple missteps and stresses:

- Outie feels embarrassed or frustrated about innie's need for solitude.
- Outie tunes out the innie's needs.
- Innie wants a voice or more independence, which outie resists.
- Outie gets angry about innie's disinterest in socializing and entertaining.
- Outie focuses too much on career or outside activities.
- Innie wants more intimacy and outie wants less intimacy.
- Innie feels ignored, unheard, and hurt.

FILMS WITH INNIE FEMALES & OUTIE MALES

Movies help us see our behaviors (and our partner's) without feeling so defensive; they help us realize that all humans do silly and frustrating things. A fun way to look at your relationship issues is to watch movies where the lead characters are a female innie and a male outie. Establish a weekly or occasional film night and, over the course of a few weeks, watch some or all of the movies listed below and discuss your reactions (these are just a few films that have sparked interesting discussions; we offer more suggestions on our Web site, www.hiddengifts.net). Use the films to understand yourself and your partner better. Discuss how the character temperaments impact their relationships. Ask yourself questions like the following: Were you attracted to a quiet but lively innie woman who listened to you? Did you feel protected and excited by your outie guy? What relationship dance steps did your parents perform? How did you feel about them? Share your thoughts and feelings with your partner and ask for his or her reactions. Make some popcorn and settle in.

Mr. and Mrs. Bridge, with left-brained outie Paul Newman as a traditional husband acting more like a father in his marriage to right-brained innie Joanne Woodward

When Harry Met Sally, with left-brained innie Meg Ryan and left-brained outie Billy Crystal evolving from friends to lovers

Titanic, with right-brained outie Leonardo DiCaprio rescuing left-brained innie Kate Winslet

Two for the Road, with left-brained outie Albert Finney growing apart from his right-brained innie wife Audrey Hepburn over the years of their marriage. If you watch only one of these films, this is the one to choose.

Something's Gotta Give, with right-brained innie Diane Keaton dipping into the world of dating and choosing left-brained outie

Jack Nicholson over the left-brained innie Keanu Reeves (go figure!)

Tangoing Twosome: Extrovert Female & Introvert Male

Remember watching *Gone With the Wind* and silently yelling "No, no, no" when Scarlett O'Hara throws herself at Ashley Wilkes? It's just so apparent that extroverted Scarlett would mow over introverted Ashley in no time at all, and that she would always feel frustrated with him. Fortunately, Ashley, a typical introvert, shows great restraint and declines. He later happily marries another innie, Melanie. Obviously, extroverted Rhett, the "he-man," is just the guy for Scarlett. So Rhett pursues Scarlett, and you know what happens next. As you can see, two extroverts are hard to domesticate.

NEGATIVE PERCEPTIONS

Unfortunately, male innies are usually seen in a more negative light than female innies are. Avril Thorne and Harrison Gough (1999) conducted a study in which they looked at how people assign traits to behaviors. The observers followed groups of ten college students around for three days. The students were interviewed several times; given personality tests; and observed during meals, in leaderless discussion groups, and during role-plays. Observers who knew nothing about the students were asked to assign traits to each student's behaviors. Extroverted males and females were described as unusually self-confident, demonstrating good social skills, capable of dealing with any situation, creating a good impression, and looking stable. Female innies were described as calm, deliberate, reserved, complicated, reflective, quiet, sensitive, retiring, lazy, imaginative, and original. (Lazy was the worst trait they were assigned!) Male introverts with the same behaviors as female introverts were assigned less-flattering traits. Innie males were described as weak, feminine, snobbish, suspicious, self-absorbed, dreamy, touchy, aloof, cautious, and serious.

Another study about marital satisfaction (Marioles, Strickert, and Hammer 1998) followed couples over seven years to monitor marital behavior, satisfaction, and divorce. Among the couples they studied, introverted men tended to marry later and, like Ashley, they usually paired up with introverted women. The study also found that extroverted women married to introverted men were the least satisfied. Clearly, these cultural influences filter down into our relationships, even without our realizing it.

The difficulties faced by this type of pair are based, at least in part, on the negative way introverted men are seen in our culture. However, all is not lost. An introvert male and extrovert female can be a good match when each partner's strengths and challenges are appreciated. Partners can then rise above the negative stereotypes and offer each other valuable qualities.

—Cultural Differences: East Meets West—

In many cultures, including ours, the male is expected to be an outie, and innie males are often devalued. However, cultural influences on individuals aren't always negative. We interviewed Jackie and Jay, who met when Jackie was a new immigrant from China and working as a waitress in a relative's Asian restaurant where Jay ate regularly. Jackie was quiet because she spoke little English. Jay, who isn't Chinese, was in a comfortable and familiar setting with people he knew, so he was chatty and friendly. From all appearances, Jay was extroverted and Jackie was introverted. However, looks can be deceiving. As she began to improve her command of English, her true extroverted temperament surfaced. And Jay, in unfamiliar settings, showed his introverted stripes. They have now been married for almost thirty years.

Jackie, as an extreme extrovert, enjoys doing the talking, being the center of attention, and focusing on her career. Jay is happy to remain in the background. He recognizes her talents, calms her down when she loses her temper, and supports her career. He feels valued because she counts on his calm manner and his tips about how to cope with Americans. And in turn she expands his social activities and brings excitement to his life.

Because of her Asian background she views his introverted qualities in a more positive light. In her country of origin, she was discriminated against and put down because of her outgoing manner. She had trouble paying attention in school and, since she came from a highly educated family, her learning struggles left her feeling humiliated and dumb. Yet, when her family immigrated to the States, Jackie, without a college education, worked her way up in her company to her present position as a vice president. As you can see, a great deal of our feelings of satisfaction come from our expectations and perceptions—when our perceptions of a particular behavior or trait are positive, we can more easily accept that behavior and build a positive relationship.

This type of relationship can offer partners a way to use their individual strengths to balance their relationship, as shown in the list below.

When this couple's strengths are in tune:

- Outie female isn't dominated by innie male.

- Innie male doesn't need to be driven or competitive.

- Outie can focus on her career.

- Outie can shine.

- Innie may enjoy unconventional roles like being a stay-at-home dad.

- Innie male is more attuned to the relationship.

- Outie feels nurtured and cared for.

- Both have freedom from traditional role expectations.

When this couple missteps and stresses:
- Innie's self-esteem is weakened as a result of being viewed in a negative cultural light.
- Outie may feel embarrassed about her partner's nonmasculine image.
- Outie sees innie as weak, a poor provider, or unassertive.
- Innie sees outie as overbearing and competitive.
- Outie feels unprotected.
- Innie may feel powerless, emasculated, and steamrolled.
- Outie may not sufficiently encourage innie.
- Innie male may feel threatened or resentful because of outie's higher income.
- Outie may not be sensitive to innie's intimacy needs.
- Outie may unconsciously resent feeling dependent on partner's stability.

FILMS WITH OUTIE FEMALES & INNIE MALES

Listed below are several films in which the lead characters are a female outie and a male innie. We've noticed that plenty of films with this kind of dynamic have come out in recent years, probably because these relationships go against the cultural grain and therefore make for great drama. Watch one or all of these movies over a few weeks and discuss how these issues affect you. Ask yourself questions like the following: Were you attracted to an energetic woman who got you out of your rut? Did you feel listened to and understood by your innie guy? What dance steps did your parents perform? How have they affected you? Share some of your observations with your partner.

The Way We Were, with right-brained innie Robert Redford feeling overwhelmed by left-brained outie Barbra Streisand

Pretty Woman, in which right-brained outie Julia Roberts brings left-brained innie Richard Gere to life

Ordinary People, with left-brained outie Mary Tyler Moore shutting out her left-brained innie husband, Donald Sutherland

Barefoot in the Park, in which left-brained innie Robert Redford tries to keep up with his right-brained outie wife, Jane Fonda

My Big Fat Greek Wedding, in which right-brained outie Nia Vardalos breaks out of her rut and finds right-brained innie John Corbett

Cha-cha-ing Same-Sex Couple

Of course, all of the differences we have discussed crop up in same-sex couples, too. This couple already faces discrimination, so adding other challenges like a difference in temperament can be stressful. Being part of a gay couple can bring unwanted attention, which many innies shrink from. Introverted gay men may face rejection from extroverted partners who idealize outgoing temperaments. Differences can mount up and become so overwhelming that they aren't discussed. Conflicts, especially in lesbian relationships, may be avoided or buried. Most gay guys have an easier time arguing, but they are more likely to freely hurl negatives at each other. Also, same-sex couples often can carry heavy loads of unconscious prejudice and shame. Those burdens can flood a relationship until it becomes a damaging toxic spill. For these reasons, it's particularly important for same-sex couples to shine a light on their differences and conflicts.

Paul Tieger and Barbara Barron-Tieger (2000) discuss their relationship research in *Just Your Type*. Their findings suggest that the more similarities couples have, the more satisfied they are with their relationships. Same-sex couples face challenges because they often have numerous differences, including age, race, and class. These differences add up. Studies (Connolly 2005) report that couples with age differences are discriminated against just as strongly as couples with other "hot" issues like homosexuality and race. Any of these differences, as Marti has seen in her psychotherapy practice, can make it difficult for one partner to understand the other. Facing so many differences, same-sex innie and outie partners may find their temperament differences even more frustrating.

Making matters more complicated is the fact that, since both partners probably grew up in homes with male-female relationships, they lack role patterns to follow. This gives them freedom from traditional role expectations, but it also causes a huge energy drain because there are few automatic expectations regarding who will do what. Everything must be negotiated. On the other hand, Marti has noticed that temperaments can actually guide couples in assigning who does what. For example, innies are often good at planning for trips and other activities in the future, and outies can encourage going to social events. In this case, a couple can be more accepting of temperament differences since they actually reduce conflict and make life easier.

Since same-sex couples aren't given the cultural sanction of marriage, they may find that developing their own personal rituals helps them maintain and support their commitment (Patterson 2005). Temperament can play a major role here too. Innies usually enjoy establishing traditions, and outies can invite friends they meet to help celebrate these new traditions. Gay people who live far from their families or who have been rejected by them find it important to build strong relationships and a sense of community. Innie and outie talents can help them to do just that.

Same-sex couples may encounter less discrimination today in some ways—but there is still plenty out there. Seeing a gay couple really triggers some heterosexual folks' primitive lizard brain and its fear of "otherness" ("They aren't like us, so they are threatening"). One of the best ways couples can counteract this hostile response is by giving themselves an antidote: they can inoculate themselves with a safe, understanding, and nurturing relationship.

FILMS WITH SAME-SEX PARTNERS

Have a flick night and watch how temperament influences the relationships in the films listed below. Although some of the characters in these films are exaggerated, the portrayals still capture struggles many same-sex couples face. Which character is right-brain dominant, and which is left-brain dominant? What other differences create challenges for the partners? Does race play a part? Illness? Social status? What advantages do the partners enjoy because of the differences between them? How do they resolve their differences? What happens if they aren't resolved? Discuss your observations and feelings about these films, and see how they relate to your own relationship.

> *Philadelphia*, with right-brained innie Tom Hanks showing strength and vulnerability with right-brained outie partner Antonio Banderas

> *The Hours*, with right- and left-brained and innie and outie partners dealing with central issues like attachments, separateness, life, and death

> *Four Weddings and a Funeral*, with right-brained innie Simon Callow giving one of the most touching eulogies ever written, about his lover, left-brained outie James Fleet

Far from Heaven, with right-brained innie Julianne Moore coming alive in 1950s suburbia and facing the coming-out of her left-brained outie husband, Dennis Quaid

The Birdcage, with left-brained outie Robin Williams trying to pass off his partner, right-brained outie Nathan Lane, as a woman

Same-Temperament Couples

Because same-temperament relationships aren't as common as innie-outie ones and are not the primary focus of this book, we'll only briefly touch on each type here.

BALLET DUET: INNIE-INNIE COUPLE

In Marti's own research about introverted and extroverted relationships, she found that the innie-innie couples reported the most relationship satisfaction of all the variety of couple combinations. A high level of satisfaction in this type of relationship makes sense, since they tend to have fewer daily conflicts than couples of different temperaments. Two innies know, of course, that you stay home on Friday night. What's often interesting about innie-innie couples is how they met. If they didn't stumble upon each other at work, they were usually introduced by a friend or relative. Without an outie to pull them out and speed up the romance, innie couples tend to have a slow-paced courtship, sometimes never marrying. Slowly this pair finds that they understand each other, that they are compatible, and that they have few conflicts. But they can become too comfortable, rely on each other too much, and get stuck in a rut. They may reinforce each other's limitations and become reluctant to stretch themselves. If you're in an innie-innie relationship, you might find it beneficial to watch some of the following movies featuring introverted couples. Watching and talking about the films encourages understanding and appreciation about your relationship.

Films with Innie-Innie Partners

Doctor Zhivago, with right-brained innies Omar Sharif and Julie Christie experiencing unrequited love due to the Russian Revolution and social restrictions

Sense and Sensibility, with right-brained innie Hugh Grant slowly uncovering love with left-brained innie Emma Thompson

One True Thing, with right-brained innie Meryl Streep as a home-maker who loves her flawed family, including her alcoholic left-brained innie husband, William Hurt

Chocolat, in which right-brained innie Juliette Binoche whips up magical love potions for right-brained innie Johnny Depp

SWING-DANCING PAIR: OUTIE-OUTIE COUPLE

An outie-outie pairing is one of the most problematic. It's fun, excit-ing, and full of dopamine—while it lasts. Imagine attempting to tie two tigers together by their tails. Two outies living together may find it hard to pause long enough to discuss and reflect on their lives and their priori-ties. The relationship will veer off course if they don't share their interior worlds—without intimate discussions the connection frays and breaks. They become roommates passing in the night. The flame fizzles out.

However, many of these couples buzz right along if they stay active. A common hobby, interest, or occupation, or even the task of raising children, can strengthen their bond and keep them moving. However, if either wants to slow down or increase their intimacy, the relationship may become strained. Marti has worked with couples, like Mary and Ken, who kept a calendar that would choke a horse. When their kids left home they felt uneasy about those blank spots in their schedules. What should they do with all that energy? They began to go on ecotours to exotic locations, signed up for tango lessons, and learned to play golf (as you might guess, they don't use the cart).

Invite some friends over and watch some films featuring outie pairs. Discuss their strengths and limitations. What works and where do they get into trouble? But no matter what happens, they always have lots of action, don't they?

Films with Outie-Outie Partners

Singin' in the Rain, with right-brained outie Gene Kelly finding harmony with left-brained outie Debbie Reynolds

Gone With the Wind, in which right-brained outie Clark Gable tries to tame left-brained outie Vivien Leigh

Terms of Endearment, with left-brained outie Jack Nicholson spinning around with left-brained outie Shirley MacLaine

Bonnie and Clyde, with quick-drawing left-brained outie Warren Beatty causing commotion with left-brained outie Faye Dunaway

Exercises: Learning New Steps— Tangos, Not Tangles

When you complete the exercises below you will better understand the differences between your partner and yourself.

Different Differences

To begin this exercise each person might go to a quiet location and respond separately to the seven statements listed below.

We are different in these five ways: _____.

I like these two differences: _____.

I dislike these two differences: _____.

How do we or could we find ways to compromise about what we dislike? _____.

I like the way we handle this difference: _____.

This is what I like about you being an innie: _____.

This is what I like about you being an outie: _____.

Then come together again and listen to your partner's answers. Discuss both of your answers without criticizing each other. Remember that you and your partner are showing trust and vulnerability when you discuss your responses. If your differences cause unresolved conflicts, flip to chapter 9 and read about "undressing" the stress. Keep in mind that differences aren't all bad. They encourage you to foster new growth in your relationship. They are the spice of life.

Discover Your Relationship Values Together

A study on marital values (Klohmen and Shanhong 2005) found that newlyweds who have similar values report happier marriages. Although most couples may not discuss or even be aware of what they value before getting serious, these beliefs have a large impact on a relationship's success. Knowing your values is your compass and guide. Differences underlie values, which in turn create expectations. When you know what is important to you and your partner, conflicts are reduced, decisions are easier, priorities are clearer, and energy isn't wasted on things that aren't meaningful or significant. Pick five values and share them with your partner. Use them to guide your decisions.

You may find it helpful to take a walk or go out to dinner and discuss what each of you values in your relationship. Values aren't right or wrong; they simply signify what is most important to you. See if you can both stay curious and leave criticism behind when you talk about the other's personal values. What relationship values did you grow up with? Also, keep in mind that words never have just one meaning—they signify different things to different people. It is important to clarify the meaning of the words you are using. For instance, "value" is a word with many meanings. Your values guide your choices and decisions, while what you value in your relationship are the elements in that relationship you appreciate or treasure.

Values come in all shapes and stripes. Perhaps you value honesty, financial security, supporting your careers, fidelity, increasing family time, or having more or less personal time. None is better than the others. Below are a few values that couples often mention. We hope this list helps you become aware of your own guiding values. Don't forget that they are often changing.

Female innies value:

Time for solitude while her outie partner is pursing his career and interests

An action-oriented partner who provides a reliable family life

Predictable, defined partner roles so that she can conserve her energy, provide stability, and maintain harmony

Being acknowledged for her efforts in taking care of home and children because her partner sees these roles as her job and appreciates her skills

Her partner's ability to pull her out into the world

Male outies value:

The parenting and homemaking skills of his partner

A home base to return to, yet lots of freedom

The limelight

Feeling calmed and listened to by his spouse

Feeling admired for his action-oriented abilities

Not having to adapt much, since his innie partner doesn't want conflict

---

It's never too late to clarify your values or update them. Ask your partner for something based on your values. For instance, if you want more time together, ask for a Friday night date. When you and your partner are aware of your values, it makes it easier to ask for what you need and want. Understanding and clarifying your values will increase your marital satisfaction. This is another way to design just the right steps for your unique couple dance. ♡

4

becoming bilingual
speaking innie and outie

"In every house of marriage there's room for an interpreter."
—Stanley Kunitz

It's ten o'clock at night and Mike enters the bedroom talking in an excited tone. "What do you think about adding three days to our vacation? I've been reading about a wonderful historic mountain house resort on the Internet, in upstate New York. It's just an hour's train ride outside of the city. I have the reservation agent on hold. What do you think?" Marti feels steam rising in her brain and escaping from her ears. "Here we go again," she thinks. Marti has told Mike at least a hundred times that she doesn't like to discuss or try to make snap decisions late at night. "Let's talk this over in the morning," she says, trying to keep irritation out of her voice. Mike says, "Okay." He leaves the room mumbling, "It's just a quick choice. Why can't we just discuss it?"

Mind the Gap

Who communicates exactly like you do? Who agrees with everything you think? Who feels the same way you do? Only one person speaks your language just exactly like you do, and that's you!

Unless you have found that magical clone of yourself, your spouse will be speaking his or her own tongue, which will likely be quite different from yours. No combo proves this point more than an innie-outie pair. As Jane Jones and Ruth Sherman say in *Intimacy and Type* (1997), "The effects of being extroverted or introverted seem to have more impact on communication problems than do any other preference."

Introverts and extroverts live in opposite worlds. Each world has its own language and styles of relating. As a result, misunderstandings occur, and gaps of miscommunication develop. However, good communication can close the gaps before they become gulches. Extroverts can learn to speak innie and introverts can learn to speak outie. Learning each other's language, or becoming bilingual, is vital to maintaining a good relationship.

Couples often get into trouble because they *expect* their partner to speak exactly like they do. Without even realizing it we may try to mold our partner into a clone of ourselves ("You should listen like I do," or "You should answer quickly like I do"). Of course, we can't and won't ever understand each other perfectly. However, it helps if we speak each other's language so we can build bridges between our two worlds. Of course, even if we become bilingual we won't eliminate glitches, because the same words can have different personal meanings. Healthy relationships are created when partners learn basic language skills that allow them to explore the other's personal meanings. Willingness to become bilingual honors one's partner's native tongue, reduces misunderstandings, and strengthens the bonds of intimacy.

SAY WHAT?

After trust, communication is the most important aspect in relationships (Kirby, Baucom, and Peterman 2005). But why? Well, we can't really become a loving couple without lowering our shields and sharing ourselves with our partner. We can't understand each other without understanding what our partner is saying. Lowering our shields and peeling off our armor allows intimacy. Intimacy offers the opportunity to know each other deeply. We can share our desires, emotions, opinions, hopes, and fears. We can clear up anger, hurts, and disappointments. Good communication gives partners the chance to understand each other, learn from their separate viewpoints, and support each person's growth. And, on a practical level, good communication helps to smooth out the day-to-day details of life quickly and accurately.

BUILDING BRIDGES

What does communicating really mean anyway? When a couple is communicating, they are building communication lanes, like a bridge, between them. A message travels back and forth between the two people in a complete loop. But communication only occurs when it goes both ways, as in the following scenario: One person sends a message and another person receives it. The receiver decodes the meaning of the words. The receiver sends a response back, perhaps a question clarifying the message received. For example, Will might say to his wife, Taylor, "I want to make sure I understood you—you are concerned about having enough time to finish your project. Did I get that right?" Taylor might reply, "Almost. I'm worried about getting it organized and finished." If we don't check the meaning of the messages we receive, misunderstandings quickly arise. And if the receiver doesn't respond, it is not a complete loop, so the pair isn't really exchanging messages; instead, they're engaging in one-way communication. Usually outies are better at the "sending messages" part of the loop and innies are better at the "receiving messages" part of the loop. When a pair establishes a sturdy bridge where they both send and receive, they have the lanes they need for helpful communication. Most conflicts can be discussed, understood, and worked through. If your communication bridge is blocked, traffic only goes one way, or misunderstandings are not checked out, then messages can't flow back and forth. Communication gets mucked up. And, to make matters even more complicated, verbal communication is just half of the story.

NONVERBAL COMMUNICATION

Every day we communicate on many levels. Verbal communication is the most common. It is necessary because we aren't born with built-in crystal balls or antennae. We can't guess another person's thoughts even with an aluminum hat on, and they can't guess ours. Yet all of our behavior communicates. We convey nonverbal information about ourselves in various ways. We send messages by our speech, silence, body language, tone of voice, pacing, timing, behavior, focus, intention, and inflection. We also communicate through writing, drawing, dancing, music, and other creative arts. The left brain attends to what words are actually spoken, puts them in order, and makes logical sense out of the message. The right brain picks up nonverbal metacommunications (meaning all of the ways we communicate) like tone, inflection, and underlying feelings and tries to make sense of the message and the medium. Sometimes you can feel something about what someone is saying, but the feeling does not agree with the actual spoken words. It is good to know whether you and your partner are right- or left-brain dominant because these tendencies affect good communication. For example, right-brained people usually talk about all their thoughts and feelings before getting to the point. Left-brained people get right to the point and then want to move on quickly. To recall your and your partner's hemisphere preference, look over the list of right- and left-brain dominance traits in chapter 2.

View from the Other Shoes

Introvert and extrovert communication styles are so different that they often appear inconsistent, confusing, or irritating to someone with the other temperament. Innies feel that their outie partners spend their relating energy out in the world. Outies often feel that their innie spouses spend their relating energy internally. Both may feel that their partners don't save much of their relating energy for them. It's hard to understand these opposing styles unless we develop empathy, by stepping into each other's shoes. Let's listen to how an outie, Hannah, and her innie partner, Matthew, perceive and misperceive each other. Notice the assumptions, often incorrect, they make about each other. When they discuss the view from their own shoes it clarifies and improves the traffic flow on their communication bridge.

Hannah: If I ask you something and you pause before answering me right away, I think you don't want to say what's on your mind. I begin to think you are keeping secrets or that I can't trust you. I think that you must be deliberately withholding something. Or, if you don't answer at all, I might think you are ignoring me. Sometimes if you are quiet I think you are agreeing with me, only to find out later that you aren't. I don't feel I can trust you.

Matthew: This is my internal experience: When you ask me a question, I receive it and inside my mind a Magic 8 Ball is turning over. I wait for the answer cube to float up. Lots of times it reads, "Ask me again later," so I have to wait again. Finally, later that day or perhaps even the next day, an answer pops into my mind. Occasionally, I am chatting away in my head. I think I have answered you when I haven't. If I am quiet, I am still thinking but not necessarily agreeing. It has nothing to do with being trustworthy, withholding, or ignoring you.

Hannah: You are very puzzling to me. I don't understand why you aren't warmer and more talkative at parties like you are at home. You seem so different in public. Sometimes I feel embarrassed when you don't contribute or you aren't very friendly.

At home, I also feel like I need to draw you out. I don't always know when you want to talk. I never know if lots of information will fall out of you or nothing at all.

Matthew: I do appreciate being asked for a comment at times because I hate to interrupt party patter. Sometimes I have something to say and sometimes I don't. At parties, it takes all my energy to absorb what's going on. Sometimes it's hard to hear because it's noisy and everyone is talking at once. I am embarrassed because I can't keep up with the chatter. If I'm tired I also try to tune out all the static in my head. I forget to smile since I am concentrating so much on trying to hear. At home, it does help if you ask me when we could talk so I'm prepared.

Hannah: I don't know why you don't want to blow your own horn. I'm proud of you and I want to brag about your achievements. Sometimes I feel like I need to tell everybody about who you really are and what you have accomplished to make up for your reserved demeanor.

Matthew:	I know I feel uncomfortable when you tell strangers about me. I feel like I'll be overwhelmed by questions that I won't be able to answer and that I'll feel stupid.
Hannah:	I get excited and I want you to share the excitement with me.
Matthew:	Sometimes I feel like you bug me. I feel like retreating. When I feel that you are in my face, pressuring me, words disappear in my brain. I can't help clamming up. I feel that I tell you what's bothering me but it doesn't seem to stick in your ears. I don't feel as if you listen or remember what I said. My experience is that you ask me something and then ignore my answer. I wonder if you are lying, because you say one thing one day and then do something else the next day. It's frustrating for me because I feel like I am always on shifting sands with you. I'm not sure I can count on you because you're always changing your mind.
Hannah:	My mind flits from one thing to another. Sometimes I forget what I was thinking earlier.
Matthew:	Sometimes it seems to me that you are focused only on superficial subjects. I wish you cared more about the deeper meanings in life. I don't care about *People* magazine. I feel embarrassed when you interrupt people and ask what I consider personal questions.
Hannah:	It's fun for me to hear about other people's exciting lives. I am interested in the lives of people I meet. I interrupt because I want to tell them something about me that relates to what they are saying.

Sound familiar? If couples assume that they know what their partner means, they end up constructing mistaken intentions. They can become frustrated and disheartened. Outies may feel like they have uncommunicative albatrosses around their necks. Their partners appear to be withholding and disinterested. Innies may feel that their partners don't value or appreciate their interior worlds. But if outies do listen carefully they will gain rich insights from their innie partners. And innies who let their partners help them to loosen up learn to enjoy the lighter side of life.

Innie & Outie Communication Strengths

Both innies and outies have communication strengths. As we have discussed earlier, each builds one directional lane on the two-lane communication bridge. Innies offer listening skills and the ability to deepen conversations. Outies can shoot the breeze with almost anyone, so they can fill in during awkward silences. Your innie-outie relationship improves when you become bilingual and learn your partner's verbal and nonverbal styles.

LEARNING INNIE

Introverts have their own unique communication strengths. An introvert's favorite expression is "Let me think about that." Their conversation style is slow, quiet, and calming. Information is taken in and responded to after careful and thoughtful consideration. Contributing to the communication loop by listening attentively without interrupting is their forte. After reflection, innies offer well-thought-out and insightful comments.

Innies:

- Listen to understand

- Have a calm and quiet presence

- Give well-thought-out responses

- Reflect in order to integrate complex information

- Don't tell tall tales

- Have deep interests so they are interesting to talk with

- Remember what others say

- Listen without interrupting

- Observe a lot and have delayed responses

- May not disclose their true thoughts or feelings unless asked

- Usually have a good sense of humor

- Like e-mail, notes, and letters

- Give feedback later about what you have discussed

How to Speak Innie

Part of learning to speak the innie language is to find the keys to unlock your innie partner's tongue. Here's how you can encourage your innie to unlock his or her lips: When you're talking with him or her, give your innie partner good eye contact and listen. Expect silent spaces between comments; don't let your mind wander during the silence. You will need to turn down your enthusiasm and speak less. Slow down your pacing, pause, lower your voice, sit back, and don't crowd your partner.

Don't finish your partner's sentences or interrupt; otherwise, your partner may not find his or her place again. It's crucial to build trust by respecting his or her privacy and confidentiality. Check with your innie before disclosing anything he or she tells you to someone else—you and your partner may have very different ideas about what's private.

Make a specific time to chat at least fifteen minutes together every day. Give your innie partner any information beforehand so he or she can preprocess it. Choose a time when you are both recharged. Chat in a quiet place without distractions—tell the kids that this is your parent talk time and not to interrupt.

Introverts value words and they like to communicate for the purpose of understanding. During your scheduled chat, take a breath, relax, and practice the fine art of listening. Reflect back what you hear your partner saying. Ask questions that will deepen the discussion. Innies feel heard if you summarize their thoughts and feelings; for example, you might say, "So, if I heard you correctly, you have been thinking about what bothers you about our kitchen. You don't want to spend much money to fix it up. You are wondering if a new coat of paint would help. Was I in the ballpark?" Let your innie respond to your summary while you zip your lip. Try not to pressure your partner for words or decisions or subtly imply that he or she should pick up the pace. Ask for your partner's opinion and then be quiet. Agree on a hand signal that he or she can use to stop you if you interrupt, such as holding up a hand with the palm out (this type of signal won't interfere with his or her process of formulating responses). When you speak, remind your partner that you are brainstorming aloud. Stay on one topic at a time, think before speaking, and speak slowly. Remember, your partner may not show his or her thoughts and feelings, but that doesn't mean there isn't a lot of listening going on. In a day or two, ask your innie partner for any further thoughts or feelings he or she may have.

—Key Points for Speaking Innie—

- Allow time to get to know your innie.

- Ask and then listen.

- Discuss one thing at a time.

- Communicate in writing.

- Expect a need for reflecting time and delayed responses.

- Match the innie's pacing.

- If the innie is slow to respond, don't interpret it as agreeing or a lack of interest.

- Arrange quiet settings for one-on-one conversations.

- Invite responses, such as "What is your thinking about this?" and "How does that seem to you?"

- Wait for an answer or ask him or her to get back to you.

Daily Interactions with Innies

Here are some suggestions for specific interactions that arise during the day. Outies will find these tips useful in their own relationships and when they are interacting with other innies.

Greetings

- Use a quiet, friendly tone.

- Disclose something about yourself, such as "I know what you mean. I love traveling."

- Do low-key connecting with some eye contact.

- Use a slow, calm pace; don't rush the greeting.

Receiving Information

- Don't rush them, and don't assume.

- Don't interrupt or fill pauses.

- Use head nods and say things like "Uh-huh."

- Speak with an upward inflection.

- Show appreciation by saying things such as "Thanks for sharing that."

- Clarify meanings by saying things like "Did you mean . . .?"

Working on a Task Together

- Have a helpful attitude and say that you enjoy working together.

- Be alert to the innie's need to process information and ask questions.

- Discuss what you are doing together; reduce small talk.

- Be careful not to intrude on the person's space.

Giving Feedback or Answering Questions

- Take it slow, and listen.

- Don't finish his or her sentences.

- Reflect back to your conversation partner what you have heard, and check it out to make sure you understand.

- Say things that make it clear you're listening, such as "Oh" and "So" followed by a pause.

- Answer questions honestly and openly.
- Acknowledge his or her point and then suggest another view.

Asking an Innie to Do Something

- Ask the innie directly to give his or her input.
- Tell the innie that you would appreciate his or her help.
- Allow the innie time for considering.
- Be supportive of his or her yes or no response.

Leave-Taking

- Use caring and gentle friendliness.
- Gently close the conversation.
- Say good-bye and perhaps set another date to get together.
- Acknowledge appreciating your talk together.

LEARNING OUTIE

Many outies' favorite expression is "Let's talk this over." Outies are active, expressive, energetic, and enthusiastic. They shoot from the lip about almost anything. Interacting with ease, they leap around a variety of subjects in group discussions without raising an eyebrow. Seldom are they at a loss for words. It's easy to "get" them. They contribute to the communication loop by sending a flow of messages, although these messages are sometimes contradictory. Their brains are wired in such a way that they think while they are talking—it is how their brains work.

Outies:

- Communicate for stimulation

- Are expressive and reactive

- Speak and act first, and think later

- Jump from subject to subject

- May not remember what is said

- Know lots of topical information

- Are masters at "conversation lite" and party banter

- Have active, spontaneous, lively, and enthusiastic energy

- Are fun loving and open about themselves

- Fill in awkward gaps in conversations and are uncomfortable with silences

- Offer lots of information without being asked

- Usually like instant messaging, cell phones, land phones, and in-person conversing

How to Speak Outie

An innie may need to refuel before engaging an extrovert in conversation. But remember that you don't have to say a lot; you just have to pump up your responses. When conversing with an outie, let the outie talk. Lean forward and give some obvious cues that you are listening, like smiling, nodding, and making good eye contact. Say things like "Go on," "Oh," "I see what you mean," and "Could you say a bit more about that?" Don't edit yourself, and occasionally respond spontaneously with enthusiasm. Speak louder and faster than you usually do. Don't allow long pauses. Use short sentences, such as "So you are saying . . . ?" Give verbal responses, feedback, and acknowledgment, such as "Wow, that's really cool." Ask questions and offer reactions like "Oh my gosh—you're kidding." Jump with your outie from topic to topic, and don't worry about interrupting. Enjoy his or her humor and loosen up. Show appreciation about the outie's comments. Respond in the moment to any conflict that comes up.

Outies may think the other person is uncomfortable, disinterested, or incompetent if their conversation partner isn't responsive. Outies focus on their own comfort level, so if they aren't comfortable they will think that the innie is causing the problem. When you're talking with outies, alert them that you are thinking something over. Say that you will tell them tomorrow about your thoughts and feelings. Remember, outies may change their minds, so don't expect their opinions to stay the same. Outies feel heard if you show interest and excitement. Outies who are thinking out loud leave little space for innies to reflect or state their opinions. Despite this, outies usually feel that innies are holding out on them. They need outside stimulation for energy, yet they leave little room for innies to give it to them.

—Key Points for Speaking Outie—

- Let outies talk, because they think aloud.
- Know that words will flow out that may have little meaning.
- Keep the conversation going; ask questions.
- Offer to brainstorm an issue with them.
- Realize that they will cover a variety of topics.
- Their conversations will end in conclusions—sometimes.
- They may take action without informing others.

- They react to and bounce off others' actions.
- They see interruptions as additions and complementary.
- They think speed equals intelligence and good decision making.

Daily Interactions with Outies

Here are some suggestions for specific interactions between innies and outies. Innies will find these tips useful in their relationships with their partners and with other outies.

Greetings

- Use a warm, louder tone of voice than you would normally use.
- Show physical and emotional expression.
- Make positive and personal comments.
- Use open gestures, handshakes, hugs, and pats.
- Make good eye contact.

Receiving Information

- Be prepared to listen—a lot.
- Respond and show your interest.
- Ask open-ended questions.
- Speak up with an upbeat, peppy inflection.

Working on a Task Together

- Present your main points about the task, and ask for input.
- Allow time for feedback and questions; sum up after a while.
- Show appreciation for the outie's input.
- Set up a time to actually do the task or project.

Giving Feedback or Answering Questions

- Encourage outie to express thoughts and emotions.
- Be patient while outie rambles.
- Clarify the outie's main points.
- Acknowledge his or her point before adding another.
- Jump in; give comments.
- Answer in a short response.
- Reflect about what you heard the outie say.

Asking an Outie to Do Something

- Explore options, make agreements, and set deadlines.
- Set up a schedule to assess deadlines, and agree on consequences if deadlines are not met.
- Get the outie's attention; clarify that he or she heard you and agrees.

- Add elements of fun.

- Use storytelling and examples about others.

Leave-Taking

- Show warmth, respect, and admiration.

- Say that you enjoyed your time together; acknowledge the outie's input.

- Suggest getting together again soon.

- Gently close the conversation.

Barriers to Good Communication

In good relationships language and relating differences are acknowledged and honored. Most relationship problems stem from misunderstandings. Since none of us has a built-in crystal ball, it's all too easy to misunderstand our partners. The bridge between partners needs to allow for back-and-forth, flowing communication. There are many ways the flow becomes disrupted, most often by a communication barrier. Ten common communication barriers between innies and outies are listed below, along with suggestions for repairing the blockage.

MIND READING. Guessing births misunderstandings. Take time to sort out where you went off track and made assumptions, and check with your partner and clarify what he or she really meant.

DEFENSIVENESS. Feeling threatened heightens defensiveness. Respect your partner's different opinion, even if you don't agree. Listen to all ideas offered.

AGGRESSIVENESS. Becoming overbearing and wanting your own way kills a partnership. It becomes a battle for control rather than cooperation. Increase mutual understanding through cooperative communication.

PRECONCEIVED OUTCOME. You're wasting time talking together if both of you aren't mutually attempting to share, understand, clarify, or find a solution to a problem. Mutual understanding and problem solving ought to be the goal.

ADVERSARIAL ATTITUDE. Your partner is not your enemy. Communicating to prove the other wrong or with the intent to hurt one's partner is not conducive to two-way communication. Adversarial thinking assumes right and wrong and is destructive to partners working together to improve their relationships. Maybe you're both right! Move into ambiguity.

RAINING ON YOUR PARTNER'S PARADE. When you share exciting news or just an optimistic viewpoint and your partner puts it down or changes the subject, sharing stops. Don't make doom-and-gloom predictions. Join in your partner's happiness.

FEELING WRONG. Devaluing your own point of view breaks down communication. Backing down immediately without stating your own thoughts and feelings helps project that your partner is critical when he or she may not be. This behavior reduces self-esteem, reduces the chance to understand and communicate with your partner, creates residual anger, and reduces problem solving. Remember, your thoughts and feelings are not right or wrong.

DISMISSING, WITHDRAWING, OR NOT RESPONDING. No interaction can happen when one partner is shut out. If your partner won't discuss decisions, waves off differing ideas, or fails to disclose everyday or personal information, this is a serious problem. Passive-aggressive behavior is extremely destructive to healthy relationships. Be direct.

MANIPULATIVE BEHAVIOR. If discussion and communicating is used only to get what one partner wants rather than for mutual understanding and decision making, the relationship is in big trouble. Be up-front and learn to mutually give and take.

LACK OF CLARIFICATION. Misunderstandings occur in a snap if meanings are not checked out. Clarifying communication reminds you that you each have your own points of view.

Now That You Are Bilingual

Congratulations. You can both speak the other's language. We hope it helps your relationship. It certainly did in ours. Now you can think about talking in a style your partner understands. Remember that chat times for both innies and outies ebb and flow based on energy levels. See if you notice patterns. What time of day do you feel the chattiest? Do you feel more like talking on the weekend? How about your partner? What settings seem to unlock both your and your partner's jaws? Check in with each other and see if patterns emerge. Discuss the length of time you both like to engage in conversation. As we recommended earlier, find time to chat together for at least fifteen minutes (uninterrupted) each day. In bed and right before falling asleep is often a good time and place. Or you can light a conversation candle signifying talk time. Walking and talking often eases any discomfort.

It is best to start out with short chats. Extend them as you become better at listening and speaking. Remember, it's an accomplishment to communicate well. Don't criticize yourself or your partner if it's uncomfortable for one or both of you. It will get easier. Remember to check in with your partner, asking "Did I understand you correctly? You seem to be saying . . ." Respond by acknowledging your partner's feedback, saying something like "You understood everything I said, except . . ." Ask your partner what he or she heard you say, saying something like "What did you hear me saying?" Clarify any miscommunications.

Congratulate each other on your new language skills! ♡

5

to go or not to go?
that is the question

"I believe that basically people are people . . .
but it is our differences which charm, delight and frighten us."
—Agnes Newton Keith

Marti admires the way Mike shoots the breeze at parties. He can throw out a comment about any topic that pops up. Something about standing up at cocktail parties ties Marti's tongue into a knot.

Marti and her best friend talk for hours. Mike can't imagine getting so swept up in a conversation. He would start feeling antsy and thinking about what he should or could be getting done.

Myths-Taken

Innies and outies have opposing responses to the same social events. Unfortunately, our culture has elevated extroverted behavior to the cultural ideal. Most of us are mistaken about introverts, and both outies and innies usually agree that introverts are *failed* extroverts. Most don't know about the advantages that innies possess. "How can I become more extroverted?" This is a question Marti is frequently asked on radio and television shows. Both introverts and extroverts think that innies should be more outgoing, should love to party, and shouldn't want to stay home so darn much. The list of innie social "shoulds" goes on and on. Trying to reconcile innie and outie social tastes that are miles apart, and untangling the many myths that surround these tastes, can really become a briar patch for couples.

Social Needs

Let's debunk a few myths and misperceptions. It is true that innies and outies have temperaments that give them different social preferences and skills. But it's a bit more complicated than just differing social skills, because temperament underlies all mind and body functions. As we noted in chapter 2, this means that a person's temperament cuts a wide swath in their lives—and socializing is only one of those areas. Social preferences underlie choices and decisions couples make about travel, vacations, family gatherings, business obligations, friendships, and leisure activities. It also crops up in another important but often neglected social sphere— the couple's own relationship. Many couples socialize exclusively with their family, friends, and kids. They forget to have that Saturday night date with each other every once in a while.

Why is this important? Dating maintains a sturdy social connection and it is an antidote to marital stresses and strains. A sound relationship between the partners is a challenge to maintain, because introverts and extroverts are hardwired for different social lives. They find their own type of social setting satisfying and enjoyable but don't understand their partner's quite different social preferences. We frequently hear comments like "I worry about Ted because he likes to be in the garage all afternoon," and "Man, my wife can't sit still—she is always on the go." These are typical remarks reflecting opposing innie and outie social needs.

LIKING PEOPLE

As we have said, misconceptions about introverted and extroverted social tastes abound. Let's tackle a few of the biggies. One commonly held belief is that introverts don't much like other people. But being an innie or an outie doesn't influence how much we like people. The fact that outies like social events doesn't necessarily mean they like the people— they like the stimulation. Innies like people, but usually in small doses because social interaction can be draining to them.

Another misconception is that introverts don't like to talk. But temperaments don't influence how much people like to talk. Innies can talk your arm and leg off in the right circumstances, and some outies aren't as talkative as others. Contrary to public opinion, all innies are not log-cabin loners, and all outies don't love to wear lampshades. Often, however, misunderstandings based on a partner's individual social preferences become prickly patches for innie and outie couples. Frequently we hear from outies about innies, "He doesn't want to go out with other couples or have them over." From innies about outies we hear, "She never wants to do anything with just the two of us. I feel unloved."

Keep in mind your dissimilar social strengths, communication styles, and preferred social settings. Understanding and appreciating each other is like giving your relationship air, water, and light. Generally, innies take longer to get to know others, limit their social life, value privacy, enjoy leisurely conversations with people they share an interest with, and take pleasure in smaller-group activities. Outies are easier to get to know, continue to enlarge their social circle, enjoy engaging people, and enjoy lively party patter and lots of hubbub.

—Tim & Jane—

Sometimes couples try to be more flexible and agreeable in the beginning of their relationships, so their social differences aren't readily apparent. But it doesn't take long for their differences to pop up. Sometimes it turns out that the gaps in their social preferences are very wide and deep. We interviewed Tim and Jane, who had recently celebrated their golden wedding anniversary. They laughed as they said that they were both amazed that they were still married. Jane told us that as a newlywed she realized that she and her husband were socially quite different animals when they threw their first holiday shindig. The party was about an hour old when Jane paused to look around the living room and thought, "It looks like everyone is having a good time, but where is Tim?" It dawned on her that she hadn't seen Tim in quite a while. She sneaked some peeks in several rooms. No Tim. She finally checked their bedroom, where she found him kicking back, reading the latest edition of Model Train Enthusiast. *When Jane asked him if he was sick, Tim said, "No, I just needed a break." Jane had no idea what Tim was talking about. "A break from what?" she wondered. The party was going so well.*

Over the years Tim continued to duck out of parties. In fact, at their recent fiftieth wedding anniversary party, Tim disappeared as usual. Jane found him snoring in his bed only an hour and a half into the celebration. She smiled to herself because he had lasted longer than she expected. He agreed to get up and join Jane when the guests were saying good-bye. Jane and Tim have developed a mutual understanding and appreciation of their different social needs over the years. They even laugh about Tim's party breaks.

Socializing Skills

In order to survive years of social decisions based on your individual tastes, you will need to recognize, respect, compromise, and cooperate. Recognize your partner's temperament and how his or her likes and dislikes affect your shared social life. Respect your own preferences, but learn to compromise if you find that you are planting yourself in your comfort zone too often. We have received hundreds of e-mails from couples saying that when they recognize and respect their different physiologies, misunderstandings melt away. What were seen as negative qualities are now perceived as innate gifts. Shaming and blaming disappear. With their newfound understanding of each other, partners have the opportunity to combine their divergent social skills through compromise and cooperation, making a stronger relationship.

Appreciating your partner's abilities fosters a sense of partnership, boosts marital satisfaction, and increases social confidence for both of you. Social confidence means having faith in your social skills, a sense of your own social needs, and realistic expectations for yourself. In other words, Marti will not be attending any parties where the wearing of lampshades is required (we can't vouch for Mike). But we can be assured that Mike won't be living alone on an island anytime soon. Blending your social gifts enlarges and deepens your social circle and encourages both of you to stretch your wings. You can grow together.

INNIE & OUTIE SKILLS

Below are a few of the basic social skills that innies and outies possess. If we've left out a social skill that you appreciate about yourself, add it to the list.

If you're an introvert, you can bank on the following skills:

- You are a good listener and you don't interrupt.
- You remember what others say.
- You can discuss a topic in depth.
- You have interesting observations and ideas to contribute.

- You give others space.

- You are talented in the fine art of conversing.

- You are good at long-term relationships.

If you're an extrovert, you can bank on the following skills:

- You express thoughts and feelings openly.

- You love to chatter and play.

- You can jump into any social situation.

- You like a wide circle of friends.

- You enjoy others' reactions.

- You draw others out.

RIGHT-SIZED SOCIALIZING

Right-sized socializing means attempting to scale your social life (most of the time) to fit your temperament. First, it requires reading the energy level of your batteries. Next, you will need to take stock of your internal social indicator. What internal messages are your instincts or thoughts sending you about the social choices you are facing? What is your gut saying? What is your head saying? Last, you'll need to check the gauge on your external social meter. Working as a team, you can discuss your choices, decide on priorities, and finally find ways to compromise and cooperate. Right-sized socializing also alerts you to pause and notice if your life is either too routine and isolated or too revved up and spinning out of control.

Don't forget that although some social duties can't be ignored, our social activities are still basically our own choice. A social life is meant to be enjoyable and fun, not a bunch of obligations we feel pressured to meet. Also, keep in mind that a strong relationship bond is only sustained through fun, games, dating, and sharing love. So keep checking in with your spouse, and don't forget to put social energy toward your relationship.

SOCIAL BONDING IS NATURAL

Remember that one of your brain stacks is the emotional brain. It evolved to establish and maintain relationships and thereby increase your survival odds. All mammals bond in similar ways—through smells, affection, excitement, enjoyable experiences, and time spent together.

An example of mammal bonding can be seen in the behavior of our two recently adopted fluffy, sapphire-eyed Ragdoll kittens. We brought Ms. Muffin home first. She came from a suboptimal cattery (what attachment theorists would call a "traumatizing environment") that didn't hand raise their kitties. She wasn't socialized with other cats or humans. However, when we brought her home, she quickly fell in love with Mike. Since we travel quite a bit, and because this breed is very relational, our veterinarian suggested adopting another kitten as a playmate for Ms. Muffin. So, a couple of months later we brought home Miss Mittens, who had been raised in a nurturing cattery. She had grown up with more than fifteen cats and lots of TLC. Well, obviously our vet hadn't consulted Ms. Muffin, because she was not happy about the intruder. In fact, she attacked her instantly and viciously. Miss Mittens was confused and didn't fight back.

We were quite worried about our new pets and didn't know what to do, so we called a cat behaviorist. She suggested separating them for several days and putting them in different rooms linked by a door with a gap under it. She advised putting a drop of perfume on Mike and both kitties' heads. She suggested that Mike (Ms. Muffin's object of affection) select a feather toy and play with each cat every few hours. Mike would be in one room with one of the cats, playing with the other cat by dragging and poking the feather toy under the door gap. Then he would switch to the other room with the other cat and do the same thing. They both batted and pawed at the toy. They could only see the other's paws but they began to associate each other's smell with play. After they got more used to each other, Mike also fed them fancy cat food together on dishes placed side by side. In two days we saw a huge improvement. Now they groom each other (a bonding behavior), hunt toy mice together, and sleep tucked around each other in a furry circle. (You can view photos of them on our Web site, www.hiddengifts.net.) It's all right if you and your partner begin to build a closer bond by pawing at each other from under a door for a while—or by tickling each other with a feather!

Assessing Battery Levels

Confident extroverts recharge their batteries when they are out and about in the world. Their batteries are drained when they kick back and hang around the house for too long. Confident introverts, on the other hand, recharge their batteries by hanging out around the house, chilling out, and doing a whole lot of nothing. Energy is drained from their batteries when they are extroverting in the outside world. This need to recharge in completely opposite ways causes quite a few social challenges for couples. Adjustments will be needed.

DIFFERENT ENERGY NEEDS

Understanding how energy functions is imperative. (See chapter 7 for more about recharging our mysterious energy.) Energy cannot be created or destroyed. It is only transformed. When innies are out in the world spending their energy, it becomes fragmented. Fragmented energy can't be used. It must be reorganized before it can be put into use. Innies reorganize their fragmented energy during rest and relaxation. Outies' energy is reorganized and made usable during activities, interactions, and stimulation. Their energy becomes disorganized when they are alone or in a less-stimulating environment. They need action in order to transform their disorganized energy into usable fuel.

Practice paying attention to your body signals and your energy levels. Check in with yourself at regular intervals and scan your body. Innies may find this easier because they are more accustomed to noticing their internal world. Their body reactions grab their attention—they are exhausted and may be unable to concentrate, for example. Outies generally feel good and are focused externally. They may not think of checking their energy levels. They aren't as accustomed to noticing their body signals because they don't produce such dramatic reactions.

When innies' batteries are low, they have the following feelings or experiences:

- They are sluggish with low energy.
- They are confused, unfocused, or unable to think.
- They have difficulty finding words.
- They have difficulty dragging themselves out of bed.
- They feel tense, scared, headachy, or frazzled.
- They feel shut down and lack motivation.
- They are tired, shaky, irritable, or dizzy or they have stomachaches.

When outies' batteries are low, they have the following feelings or experiences:

- They feel nervous, antsy, or unfocused.
- They feel down, depressed, and yucky.
- They are frustrated or irritated easily.

- They get sick more often, overeat, and have difficulty sleeping.

- They get bored, tense, and restless.

- They feel that they have to do something—anything.

Checking Your Internal Social Indicator

After you assess your battery levels, the next step is to take an internal reading to determine whether to attend a particular event. Ask yourself the following kinds of questions: Do I have several social events scheduled on one day? Have I been to lots of social events lately? Have I been home all week? Do I have several engagements coming up? How do I feel about going to these particular social events? Am I looking forward to them?

Marti spends hours with introverted clients helping them evaluate whether to go or not to go to a social event. These decisions can be very difficult. Most folks, even extroverts, struggle with these choices, especially if we are not revealing our true feelings to our partner. The following tips can help you weed through these confusing conflicts. Remember, there is no right answer. This is *your* social life.

CAST OF CHARACTERS

Listening internally means you sit down and turn up the house lights on your internal stage. Quiet your mind and turn up the volume coming from the characters on your stage. Each character in your internal play has its own viewpoint. See if you can hear their lines, each expressing the character's individual opinions and preferences: "I love going to Fred and Carrie's. They are so much fun. But I have the open house and party on Saturday—that might be too much." "I don't want to miss out on the fishing trip." "Driving all the way to and from Fred and Carrie's will be tiring, but I would hate to miss the fishing trip that same weekend." "Man, that fishing trip with the guys sounds great."

Few choices in life are simple. We're sure you have noticed that. Contributing to the complex nature of life are the conflicting parts of ourselves that pipe up when we are making social decisions. We may be able to hear them, or it may be that their microphones are turned off, so we don't know what they think.

—Jan & Jeff—

Jan and Jeff were invited to the opening of a major museum exhibition focusing on the Lewis and Clark expedition. Unfortunately, it fell on the same night as Jeff's company holiday party. Jan, an innie, thought it over and realized that she really wanted to attend the opening, but she felt guilty about her preference. She just didn't feel as compelled as Jeff did to attend business functions. Jeff, an outie, wasn't too pleased about her choice. Jeff knew Jan hated large parties but felt she didn't understand the pressure he was under to attend his company party accompanied by his wife. He thought they should both go to the party. Besides, he didn't want to miss out on a fun time with his work pals. Jeff felt trapped and afraid. He would love to attend the exhibition, since he hated to miss this once-in-a-lifetime event, but he also thought that missing his company party could have a negative effect on his career. He didn't want to face his conflicting feelings, so he got mad at Jan. He blamed Jan for his feelings, taking it personally that she didn't want to attend his company party. For her part, Jan felt attacked for being honest about her feelings when Jeff asked her what she wanted to do. Jeff felt that Jan wasn't being supportive. Jan felt that Jeff wasn't considering her feelings. Does this sound at all familiar? It does to us!

RESOLVING CONFLICTS

Jan and Jeff's experience illustrates how conflicts about socializing develop. We all feel torn at times when we are invited to conflicting social events. Unless we definitely don't want to go, most of us resist making a choice. Many people don't want to miss out on what they expect to be a pleasurable experience. Plus, we hate to feel left out, and we don't want to offend anyone important to us. But an interesting thing happens to us humans if we don't acknowledge our conflicting internal voices. We begin to think that our partners are delivering the dialogue that is actually occurring inside our own noodles. We think our spouses are causing the problem. We feel like our partners are keeping us from doing something we want to do. We tussle with our loved ones instead of duking it out internally with our own cast of conflicting characters.

Extroverts, more than innies, tend to project their internal mixed feelings onto others. If innies are conflicted they tend to blame themselves. Moreover, innies may feel guilty about not wanting to go, being too tired to go, or having mixed feelings about going. It really takes a lot of energy and attention to listen to our own conflicting voices.

Self-awareness increases our ability to recognize our mixed voices. When we acknowledge our mixed feelings and voices speaking to us from that inner stage, we don't have as many conflicts with others, and we can solve our own conflicts. Of course, if we don't manage our mixed emotions, conflicts reoccur, as in the film *Groundhog Day*, where Bill Murray keeps reliving the same scenarios each day, never moving forward. In our previous example, if Jeff were to listen to his internal voices, he'd realize that he feels torn—he'd love to attend both events. Once he came to that realization, he would be able to discuss his mixed feelings with Jan.

Work as a team to find solutions. Accept your internal conflicts by tolerating discomfort and confusion. Knowing your thoughts and feelings is the true path to finding solutions without creating unproductive fights.

Prioritizing Social Events

Listed below are some of the questions and considerations you and your partner may take into account when prioritizing social events. Pick the ones that apply to you, ask your spouse to do the same, and set a time to discuss your priorities. Discuss your answers together. Listen to your partner's answers. Your responses will clarify conflicting thoughts and feelings that come up when you're selecting social events to participate in. Remember, you and your spouse have a right to separate opinions. Decisions aren't right or wrong. They are simply choices.

- Have you been socializing too much or too little lately?
- Are you up for this social event?
- Is this event with people you like?
- Do you enjoy this type of socializing?
- Do both of you need to attend?
- Do you really want to go?
- Did you have fun at similar events?
- Have you had company over recently?
- Is this event required for work?
- Would someone you care about be hurt if you didn't attend?
- Is this an occasion your spouse would enjoy?
- How would you feel if you didn't go?
- Are you afraid to go?
- What is the worst thing that could happen if you did or didn't go?

COMPROMISING & COOPERATING

Compromising involves discussing your preferences with a give-and-take attitude. Each of you may need to sacrifice something. Cooperating means that each of you feels you're working together toward a win-win solution. You need to do both of these things in order to come up with a solution that works for both of you.

Keep looking at alternatives. Nothing is set in stone. If you're trying to decide between two events that take place simultaneously, can you go to both for a short time? Can you go early? Can you go late? Can you skip this event even though you'd like to go? What about attending the event your partner prefers? Can you go to your choice this week and your partner's choice next week? Can you each pick one event to go to? Does your partner even want to go? Can you go alone? Can you take different cars? Can one of you ride with some friends? See how many possible compromises you can come up with. Approach decisions with an attitude of cooperation. Negotiate how long you will stay. If the two of you usually do what you want to do, try doing something your partner wants to do, and vice versa.

Add some humor and perspective to decision making by trying one of these playful ways to make choices:

- Write your choices on small slips of paper or sticky notes, attach them to a dartboard, and throw darts at them. Try it for fun. Go to the event with the most darts.

- Place your invitations in a hat and pick one or two.

- Toss a coin—heads means you go and tails means you don't.

See if you can loosen up your approach to social choices; they really aren't life-or-death decisions.

PARTY PLANNING

Getting ready to throw a party or attend one is an opportunity for conflict or connection, depending on your level of understanding, compromise, and cooperation. When preparing for a party or other social event, it is important to team up and help each other. Of course, it also makes it more fun.

Before the Party

When preparing for a party, innies can use their ingoing abilities, and outies can use their outgoing natures to encourage and support their innie partner.

> **Innies:** First, think about the upcoming party and picture yourself having a good time, engaging in chitchat with other guests. Small talk is an important part of most parties because it allows you to get to know others, even though it isn't an innie's cup of tea. Knowing that you'll need to engage in at least some small talk, mentally prepare yourself to go to the party by practicing this skill. Have your outie pick three items from the newspaper or an Internet news source: "How 'bout those Knicks?" "Can you believe how the weather is changing?" "I just saw the new Spielberg film." Together, practice talking about the three items aloud. Alternatively, think of a restaurant you might tell others about, a hobby you might discuss, or a vacation you could talk about with excitement. Remind yourself that you don't have to be a big talker. You can show interest in others by listening, nodding, smiling, and laughing too. Outies like those responses. When you need to, you can take breaks or just sit and watch the festivities for a while.

Additionally, innies don't always pick up on clues about who likes them. They can also forget pleasant experiences. So remind yourself about friends who will be at the party, and recall having had fun at a similar occasion.

Party Day

Outies: Remind your innie to rest before the party and start getting ready early. Don't add to his or her stress by rushing or running late. Agree on time commitments; estimate when you will go and when you will leave. (We always have to negotiate the times for arriving and for coming home. If the party starts at 8:00 P.M., Marti likes to arrive at 8:30 P.M. and leave around 9:00. Mike likes to arrive early to help out and stay late to clean up.) Make a compromise about how long you'll stay—but keep it open for review in case you are both enjoying yourselves. Before the party, tell your partner he or she looks attractive. When you enter the party, do not expect your innie partner to dash to the center of the crowd immediately. Allow him or her to slowly ease into the group in order to manage overstimulation. It's okay for him or her to be alone for a bit. Find a group at the party. When your partner joins in, make the appropriate introductions. Mention anything they might have in common or a topic they both could discuss. Wave or wink at him or her if your partner sits on the sidelines for a while.

Innies: Take a nap and eat some protein-rich food before going to the party. Don't rush; have the sitter arrive early if you have children. Tell your outie how great he or she looks. Take a few breaths when you arrive at the door of the party. It's okay to feel like you have butterflies fluttering in your tummy. You can always leave if the party is terrible. But you might have fun. When you enter the party, say hello and give a gift to your hostess, look at the view, if there is one, or look at family pictures lining the hall. Join others who look friendly, smile, and make casual eye contact. Ask introductory questions: "How do you know the host?" "Do you know what's in this salad?" "What do you think about this piece of artwork?" Ask questions about the topic at hand.

Remember that party groups break up every ten to fifteen minutes, so don't take it personally if the group disperses. When this happens, find a place to sit on the sidelines and take a break—pretty soon you will probably be in a deep, meaningful conversation with another innie who is also skirting the group. After a while, when you're ready, you can enter the group your outie partner is hanging with. Nod, laugh, say "Mm-hmm," and smile without showing your teeth (people unconsciously perceive teeth flashing as aggressive).

Postparty

Innies and outies: A day or so after the party, discuss what you both enjoyed or disliked about the party. Tuck these experiences into your social memory bank. This helps innies balance their tendency to remember the negatives. It also helps outies recall the event. Tell each other what was helpful or what wasn't, and keep these things in mind in the future when you are choosing and negotiating social events.

BUSINESS-RELATED EVENTS

Couples can use their individual strengths to help each other manage social issues during work functions. Our business lives often involve perplexing social and political choices. If we don't give them some thought we can get stuck in automatic ruts, saddled with unrealistic expectations and disappointments. At one extreme are the people who let their workplace become their whole social life. At the other extreme are the folks who don't think they should socialize with people from their workplace. The answer is always, of course, somewhere in the middle. Some jobs require socializing, and some don't. Put your heads together and help each other discuss conflicts and choices. Broaden your thinking and don't automatically respond. One of the advantages to being in an innie-outie relationship is that two heads and temperament viewpoints are better than one. A partnership is a good place to kick around lots of options.

Marti's career requires her to travel frequently to promote her books. As a doctor once jokingly told Marti, "Publishers try to kill authors on book tours so their work will become more valuable." We believe it. Even though Marti's publisher tried to give her more rest stops than they usually give authors (because they had read and understood the insights in her book about innies, which she was promoting), Marti didn't rest enough after the first tour. It took her about six months to recover her health and she vowed never to get that exhausted again.

Recently we both went on a rather grueling tour of the United States and Canada to publicize Marti's second book, *The Hidden Gifts of the Introverted Child* (2005). For this tour, we pooled our innie and outie talents. This time around Marti stretched out on the hotel bed in between TV appearances, radio interviews, and talks. As she lounged in the hotel room restoring her introvert's energy, Mike used his extrovert's hunger for new experiences by strolling around whatever city we were in, snapping photos for Marti to see when we returned home. He also checked e-mail, made phone calls to the publisher, made travel arrangements, and hunted down take-out desserts to bring back to the room. Although Marti missed actually seeing the sights, she was in much better shape when we returned home. It was a compromise that worked well for both of us. (However, on the next book tour Marti thinks Mike should go by himself and just bring along a blow-up doll of Marti.)

LEISURE TIME

Weekends are a time where innie and outie differences are very noticeable. Usually the amount of time for rest and socializing differs for innies and outies. Be sensitive to your own and your partner's feelings and needs, and keep in mind that different rhythms are good. It's okay to divvy up activities. And it's good to use the "a bit of this and a bit of that" approach.

Discuss your leisure time and how you both feel about it. Remember, everything can be worked out, so there's no need to fight. Ask each other what leisure activity you enjoy together. For instance, Mike and I like to walk around parks, take drives to new spots, and visit open houses. Also, ask what changes you would like to make. More time together or apart? How do you think these changes will affect your relationship?

Jack, an innie, felt he and his outie wife, Gail, didn't have much in common. When he began to go with her as she shopped at various craft stores, collecting materials for her art projects, he was surprised to find that he felt more involved with her. It led to discussions of her work in which he offered input she valued. And, although he enjoyed sailing alone he began to invite Gail to go out with him on his boat.

Jot down your different choices for activities. Pick one and dream up one creative and fun way of doing this activity that both of you will enjoy. A couple we interviewed worked out their socializing differences about throwing parties. Steve, an outie, loved to throw big bashes. His innie wife, Valerie, did not. Believe it or not, they found a way to work out this pretty big difference. They gave a huge party every six months and both felt pleasure in the event. Valerie loved to decorate, so she dolled up their house, ordered the take-out food, and played hostess. She darted around chatting with various guests. She said, "I can flit around like a butterfly." There was no pressure on her to chitchat, and she was able to control her own time, never having to land too long at one time ("Got to check on the food!" she'd say). Steve could be the social life of the party and talk to everyone.

For us, attending the ballet was a similar issue. Mike was quite surprised to find that he enjoyed the ballet performances once Marti cajoled him into going. Likewise, Marti enjoys riding shotgun in the golf cart even though she doesn't swing the clubs.

Hang your list of activities you would like to do together on the fridge. But don't forget to do some things independently. All of our married life, Marti has had female friends she gets together with each week. At first Mike felt jealous because they could chat about emotions in a way he couldn't. He used this as a signal to beef up his own ability to share personal thoughts and feelings with his male friends. We have both grown from appreciating the differences in each other.

TRAVEL & VACATIONS

Vacations are breaks from your everyday life. Anything you do that is different from your regular life is technically a holiday. Marti can feel as if she is on vacation if she checks into a hotel in her own hometown. To her it's a holiday if she orders room service, glimpses a fresh landscape from the window, and selects in-room movies.

In her first book, *The Introvert Advantage: How to Thrive in an Extrovert World* (2002), Marti describes a vacation we took together where we stopped in Leadville, Colorado. As you may have read in the book, Mike thought spending more than a week in one small city was way too long, and he wanted to drive somewhere—anywhere—for more stimulation. Marti thought it was way too short, since there were so many interesting cemeteries and lead mines to visit.

Since we have such different tastes in holidays, we have compromised during our forty-plus married years by taking turns picking vacations. This offers us new and unique trips that we otherwise would not have picked for ourselves. This year, Marti chose a historic barge cruise. Since she watched a documentary about barges on the History Channel, she has always wanted to spend a leisurely holiday floating through the canals of Alsace-Lorraine in France.

The brochure says our charming, intimate vessel will be burning up the canals at three to five miles an hour. Mike was relieved to find out that he can bike or walk alongside the barge. He had been a bit concerned about being able to stand upright in what is referred to as our "compact" cabin (the tour operators recommend a duffle bag instead of a suitcase—yet another indication of just how small our cabin may be). When we told another innie-outie couple about our upcoming barge cruise, the introvert said, "Oh, how exciting. Ever since college I have always wanted to take a barge trip." The outie partner looked at Mike and said, "I hope your marriage survives!"

When you discuss vacation plans it's important to consider all aspects of traveling. Focus on what each of you brings to the table. Outies usually bring enthusiasm and lots of information about where to go and what to do on vacation. Innies offer thoughtfulness, research ability, time limitations, money requirements, and the ability to foresee difficulties. Most innies need to pay attention to pacing; be sure to plan breaks from your jam-packed travel schedule and fast-paced sightseeing. Many extroverts want to go everywhere and see everything, but it's important to set priorities and remember that you don't need to see everything together. You may want to see some sights as a couple, some individually, and some with other traveling companions.

It's also important to discuss what type of vacation you each want when you're planning a trip. How much fuel is in your tanks as you start this vacation? Do you need lots of recharging time, or do you need more variety, more action, or a bit of this and a bit of that? Do you need to spend social time with friends and family?

It's important to think about what is motivating you to travel, because that will influence how you end up feeling about the trip. In general, innies and outies have different motivations for traveling. Outies like to share stories about their trips, have varied experiences, meet folks, try new activities, visit family, shop, eat, and gather bushels of stimulation. Innies like to experience familiar places, enjoy nature, rest, learn about something interesting, and have time alone with their partner. Discuss what inspires you to travel, both before and after your vacations. Talk about what you enjoyed, what was disappointing, what was surprising, and what you wish you had skipped. Each of you may have different opinions and feelings about the trip, and that's okay.

FAMILY GATHERINGS & HOLIDAYS

Family gatherings and holidays can ignite social stressors for innie and outie couples. Compromise, cooperation, and creativity douse the flames caused by these problems.

Marta, an innie, didn't want her in-laws to stay with her family when they came to visit for two weeks during one summer. Her husband's family members were very extroverted, talkative, noisy, and chaotic. But in their culture saying no to parents is frowned upon, and parents always stay with adult children when they visit. Marta had given in for three summers in a row, and each time the two weeks felt like two years. During her in-laws' visits, she would hide out in her bedroom or camp out at her girlfriends' as much as possible. This year, they had a new baby, and she was sleep deprived and fed up. Her husband, Augustine, an outie, felt torn between his parents and his wife. He knew his parents were irritating but he felt like he wouldn't be acting like a good son if he didn't allow them to stay at his house. He was already getting pressure from his sister and aunt. After some heated discussions between them, Marta and Augustine found a way to compromise. He would ask his parents to stay with his brother, who lived nearby, because of the baby. They would go out to dinner with his folks several times, have them over a few times (for take-out food), and Augustine would go on a couple of excursions with them. His parents weren't thrilled, but Marta was.

Outies are good at dragging their spouses out into the world. Charles, an outie, visited his family in the Southeast twice a year. One year, Charles charmed and enticed Maggie, an innie, into going with him. Maggie preferred to stay home because his rowdy family wore her out. Plus, they didn't seem very interested in her. Because Maggie was an antique collector, Charles researched antique stores in the Southern coastal area where his folks lived. In a heart-shaped box he tucked a list of antique-store addresses, a check for some mad money, and a coupon for just one dinner with his family. The creative approach worked and she went with him every year after that.

As you can see, imagination and compromise can help you solve conflicts around family gatherings and holidays and can even make them fun for both of you.

SOCIAL SET

Like salt and pepper, couples in healthy relationships preserve a feeling of separateness while forming a set or a team. It doesn't take a pair of clones for a couple to become a team. It just takes two people who both want a good, spicy relationship. Members of a healthy couple spend time alone, care for each other, and enjoy a satisfying life together.

Fun & Games

All relationships need to include some fun and games. Life has enough problems and struggles to make us all start to take ourselves and our existence too seriously. We need to balance the serious side of life with some adult playfulness. And having fun together is another way to strengthen your bond. Social researchers have found that the purpose of fun and laughter is to help people enjoy each other's company. But what is fun and games to an outie and what is fun and games to an innie may be quite different. Outies interact with the world by acting and reacting. They need to experience something in order to understand it. They often like fast-paced "face time," so play for them may mean joining a team sport, engaging in a competitive activity, attending a workshop, planning a party, or cheering their team from the grandstands. Innies, on the other hand, prefer to take in what the world has to offer, mull it over, and then act or respond after thoughtful consideration. They need to imagine and understand an experience before engaging in it. Their leisure activities tend to be more solitary or involve small groups. Hiking, reading, strolling in nature, meditating, and enjoying art are usually energizing for them.

So how can innies and outies enjoy fun and games together when their ideas of fun are so different? When we were first married we were cash-strapped college students. For recreation, we decided to put some zip in our lives and play board games every Friday night. We would even splurge on a pizza mix (this was before frozen pizza) and get out Marti's beat-up Monopoly board from her childhood. We set it up on our apartment patio table, ate some pizza, selected our shoe or race-car piece, and began the game. Right off the bat we discovered an eye opener: we didn't play with the same rules. Mike had grown up with the "take no prisoners" approach to the game and played strictly by the rules printed on the inside of the box. Marti and her friends had always made up the rules as they went along, inventing a kinder, gentler game of Monopoly. Playing by Mike's rules, Marti lost in no time at all. The following Friday night it was the same story. By the third Friday night Marti wasn't quite as enthusiastic. Being killed every game wasn't much fun for her. Mike, however, seemed to be having a gay old time, unaware that Marti was no longer laughing very much.

Mike was focused, like left-brained folks tend to be, on playing the game by the rules. Playing to him meant focusing on winning. Marti was focused, like most right-brained folks tend to be, on the process of playing the game and enjoying the interaction. Seeing Marti's discomfort, Mike shifted into a more right-brained style of playfulness over the years. And Marti gradually developed more appreciation for the value, at times, of zesty competition.

Keep Dating

Relationships stay afloat through stormy seas when partners enjoy each other's company and spend time together. Schedule a date night once a week or twice a month. Sit down and talk about some of the activities you enjoy. Jot down a few you both agree upon, and try them out. Go miniature golfing, go dancing, take a stroll, take a class, go to a lecture, go bowling, or go skating. Do something you enjoyed as a child. Try something you have always wanted to do.

Once you've decided on a few activities, jot down the dates and corresponding activities on your calendars. Keep the dates! Extroverts are easily distracted and may forget, so keep the list in a prominent place where the dates are easy to see.

Giving True Love

After a few months of having date nights, venture out of your comfort zone and learn the fine art of giving. Unfortunately, our culture promotes lots of taking or, at best, making things "even Steven" in relationships. Doing what we want to do is seen as taking care of ourselves. This attitude doesn't make for very good marriages. Occasionally doing something that your partner enjoys and you don't demonstrates unselfishness, a willingness to give of yourself, and thoughtfulness. Not only that, but it also shows your partner that you truly love and care about him or her. It makes your relationship much better.

Ask your partner what he or she likes to do—something that he or she avoids because you don't enjoy it. Perhaps your partner wants to go dancing? So go dancing. And find ways to enjoy the experience; you may enjoy dressing up, swaying to the music, holding your loved one, seeing him or her having fun, watching others, and learning a few new steps.

Then your partner can do the same thing for you—perhaps attending a baseball game or watching a car race. If loud noises are a problem, encourage your partner to bring earplugs and find ways to enjoy the spectacle: sharing your enthusiasm, critiquing the uniforms, guessing who will win, timing the pit crew, or watching the crowd. Watching a car race does not sound like fun to Marti! Luckily, Mike doesn't care for it either. ♡

pillow talk:

uncovering intimacy

"If sex is such a natural phenomenon,
how come there are so many books on how to do it?"
—Bette Midler

Lying together in the dark, cuddling, and chatting are wonderful ways to create intimacy, the superglue of relationships. These moments are usually what come to mind when we think about intimacy. However, intimacy is an often-misunderstood concept. It's really about having well-oiled adjustable armor. Seems kind of paradoxical, doesn't it?

Out in the world, in everyday life, we all need to guard our inner thoughts and feelings. It isn't good to let your boss know that you don't think much of her. Friendships last longer if we aren't always honest about our opinions—like what we think of our pal's newly remodeled black marble bathroom, especially if the pal thinks the remodel is the greatest thing since sliced bread and we think it's horrible. Ironically, for true intimacy we need to have control over our armor, like *Star Trek's* Captain Kirk issuing orders for the *Enterprise* such as "Shields up," and "Lower shields." Having adjustable armor means that our shields glide up and down according to the situation, allowing more or less intimacy in relationships. Trusted partners are invited into our inner sanctum of personal thoughts and feelings, while those we don't quite trust are kept out. Sexual intimacy involves allowing your partner into the innermost sanctum, a place deep inside that's reserved exclusively for one's loved partner. Peeling off your emotional and physical armor creates a strong and lasting bond with your partner and establishes a connection with deep roots. Intimacy also means establishing an exclusive sexual relationship. Fostering intimacy takes courage because it's an enormous challenge, like going into outer space. It's also terrifying since it triggers our lizard brain's fear of rejection and abandonment.

What Is Intimacy?

In this chapter, we will explore several areas of intimacy in an effort to find out what it really is. First, we will talk about increasing intimacy by reducing possible barriers. Second, we will take a peek at what cultivates intimacy. Third, we will discuss how touching, hand holding, back rubs, massages, kissing, and hugging increase the ability to be more intimate with your partner. Fourth, we will talk about ways to give and receive affection. And last, we will get down to the nitty-gritty—sex.

Sexuality is a very personal and private subject. When Marti works with couples she always finds that humor goes a long way toward easing the embarrassment that may accompany a sexual discussion. We found ourselves becoming silly every time we talked about this chapter. Marti kept saying she did not want to reveal anything personal. Mike kept suggesting personal details from our lives, just to shake Marti up. Needless to say, the names of the folks in this chapter have been changed in order to protect the innocent, including ourselves. We hope we can stimulate some discussion, with or without humor, between the two of you. Look over the list below and discuss the barriers you recognize. Don't blame each other—intimacy is scary for everyone. Keep a dialogue going. You may find it quite stimulating.

Reducing Barriers to Intimacy

Unfortunately, there are many barriers to sexual and physical intimacy. Reluctance to talk about secret desires or sexual needs, even with one's partner, is just one such barrier. Below are some additional reasons why introverts and extroverts have difficulty in the areas of intimacy and sexuality.

Introverts' barriers to intimacy include the following:

- Reluctance to share private thoughts and feelings
- Reluctance to share intimate sexual thoughts and feelings
- Reluctance to share physical territory
- Reluctance to talk about their needs and wants
- Being too serious about intimacy and sex
- Expecting outie partner to read innie's mind
- Blaming themselves for intimacy or sexual problems
- Discomfort with expressing anger

Extroverts' barriers to intimacy include the following:

- Not slowing down enough to share intimately
- Talking too much and not listening enough

- Getting irritated that innie doesn't talk enough
- Attempting to read partner's mind regarding his or her desires
- Reluctance to share intimate details of life
- Reluctance to be vulnerable
- Reluctance to spend enough intimate couple time
- Harboring resentments and blaming partner

LOWERING YOUR SHIELDS

Learning to comfortably lower your shields and expose vulnerable thoughts and feelings to your partner is easier said than done. Each temperament has built-in protections that need to be acknowledged and respected. Developing awareness about your protections paves the way to developing more intimate conversations. Below are some suggestions for each of you.

Increasing Intimacy with Your Innie

- Set a gentle pace. Your innie partner needs time to reflect on sexual experiences before speaking. Don't immediately ask, "How was it?"
- Schedule times to talk and focus on intimate conversations —this gives your innie time to put together thoughts and feelings.
- Listen to your innie partner's thoughts and feelings without interruption or defensiveness.
- Listen without preparing what you are going to say next, and pay attention to feelings and needs.

- Ask for and validate your partner's thoughts, feelings, and wishes.

- Take time to reflect on what your partner says. Don't dismiss a statement out of hand. Instead, take time to reflect on the conversation, and come back later for clarification.

- Don't overwhelm your partner with noise, energy, fast talking, or demanding and intrusive behavior.

Increasing Intimacy with Your Outie

- Listen without dismissing your partner's comments as superficial. An extrovert may need to talk to really get down to what is important.

- Show more expression and discuss your reactions to what your partner says—your outie partner may not be comfortable talking about intimate topics and may need encouragement to keep talking.

- Talk about what's going on with you even if you aren't clear on it yet—simply say, "I think this is what I am feeling now. I want to come back and talk later."

- Look at your outie partner, nod, smile, and tell him or her that you are quiet because you are thinking, not because you feel critical.

- Speak louder and faster. Say anything—outies want to hear something. Silence can be deadly for outies when discussing intimacy because they will fill in the blanks with negative comments.

- Practice playful responses without editing yourself.

—Ella & Nathan—

Ella and Nathan had found themselves in the same old boat once again: Nathan was angry and hurt and Ella was confused and scared. Nathan wanted to discuss the disagreement right then and there, and Ella clammed up. Ella wasn't sure what had caused the rift and she certainly wasn't ready to talk about it. She felt jumped on and pressured. Nathan tried talking and then shut down out of frustration. He felt ignored. Now both Ella and Nathan had stopped talking to each other, and both felt distant and angry.

After some time, Ella finally broke the ice and said, "I feel frustrated and alone when we aren't talking." Since she had lowered her shields and talked about her inner feelings, Nathan felt more able to take a risk, and he asked her, "Is it hard for you to talk right now? Would it be better if we talked later tonight or tomorrow?" Ella agreed, and both she and Nathan relaxed. When they met later, they were more open with each other. "I felt like you didn't care that I wasn't feeling well," Nathan told her. "I was busy getting breakfast and I didn't really notice how you looked," Ella responded. "How are you feeling now?" As a result of their exchange of feelings, both felt more understood, and they were able to make up and move on. As Ella and Nathan found, intimacy is increased and misunderstandings are reduced when you risk sharing your thoughts and feelings. Lowering your shields builds a foundation for other aspects of intimacy.

Love Potions

Since innies and outies have different emotional, physical, and intimacy needs, it's vital to understand how intimacy is created and preserved. Why do love, intimacy, and feeling connected stir pleasure? Chemicals play a large part in sparking love and keeping it alive (Slater 2006). At the beginning of a relationship, dopamine is released to ignite attraction and pursuit. It is the magic potion arousing pleasurable sexual attraction. It creates energy, exhilaration, focused attention, and motivation.

So, dopamine-driven passion fuels excitement, risk taking, boldness, and a feeling of being alive. As normal daily living with the new partner is established, dopamine production drops off. As this exciting chemical shuts down, exciting love fades. Passions wane. This may explain why divorces spike around the four-year mark. Keeping love alive after Cupid's dopamine arrow loses its power requires couples to foster the release of oxytocin, a chemical that fosters bonding and connecting. Oxytocin is released in a mother's body when she gives birth to a baby, to ensure the mother's attachment and ability to parent her new child. It also maintains love and connection throughout a long-term marriage.

KEEP THOSE CHEMICALS FLOWING

It's quite a blow to our romantic notions when we realize that long-term loving relationships are maintained by triggering the release of chemicals, isn't it? This is why it matters how we behave with our partner. Intimate, loving behavior releases pleasure chemicals, which stoke the fires of attachment. If we can't trigger these chemicals in ourselves and each other, love and caring will die out. One of the reasons that the empty-nest syndrome is so common is that oxytocin is reduced when children fly out of the nest. All marriages go through transitions and cycles. We have to fall in love with our partner over and over, again and again. During those falling-out-of-love periods we can increase our chemical links by how we treat each other and what we do together until we fall in love again.

We wonder if these chemicals may also explain some innie and outie patterns. The fact that extroverts' brains rely on the dopamine neurotransmitter may explain why outies tend to date sooner, have more affairs, and have a higher divorce rate. If a marriage lasts past the intense, dopamine-fueled honeymoon period, then the spouses must move on into the calmer oxytocin years; perhaps, when dopamine fizzles out, outies find it harder to trigger oxytocin. Innies may not find romance as quickly because they don't produce as much of the romance-inducing dopamine. But they may have an easier time triggering the release of oxytocin than outies do. We wonder if this explains why innies date later, marry later, have fewer affairs, divorce less, and maintain longer relationships in general.

Dopamine Shots

Both innies and outies can use the natural help of chemicals to keep a healthy and enjoyable relationship alive. Outies stay engaged when love is sparked by boosting dopamine. If it isn't too intense, innies can enjoy it too. Doing novel things together, exercising, dancing, going to theme parks, and surviving a natural disaster together can bring you closer (we don't recommend this one, although having lived through the Northridge, California, earthquake in 1994, we know it works). The release of dopamine may also explain why relationships begin during wars and other disasters.

Learning about the power of these chemicals allows us to see how they have affected our relationship. For instance, we met during a dance class, as dopamine was obviously shooting through us. Also, although Marti is afraid of heights she took Mike on a surprise hot-air balloon ride for our twentieth anniversary. It was new and exciting for both of us, but Marti perhaps didn't enjoy the dopamine as much as Mike did, because she spent the flight hunched low in the basket and gripping a post nearby—so much so that the balloon pilot had asked her to unclench her hand because she was accidentally squeezing the fuel line. We agree that a balloon crash would have been altogether too much dopamine for either of us.

Oxytocin Boosts

As mentioned earlier, oxytocin promotes a feeling of connection and bonding. You and your partner can stimulate the production of oxytocin by hugging, massaging each other, making love, laughing together, discussing personal details about yourselves, and sustaining eye contact.

It is especially important to do these things when children grow up and leave home, so you can maintain your intimacy and avoid drifting apart during this new phase of life.

Strokes for Different Folks

After the dating stage of a relationship, many couples forget to woo each other. Daily life can become busy and displays of affection may wane. However, relationships grow stale and strained without the chemical boost that comes from physical affection. Wooing and romance preserve strong bonds and act as a buffer against the routine annoyances of everyday life. Physical intimacy is an important way to keep the fires of love burning. And this can be a challenging area for an innie-outie pair. Innies are territorial and lose energy when others are physically close to them. Therefore, they are often slow to let others into their space. They may not be as physically demonstrative as an outie, but when they are well fueled they may enjoy touching more. Outies gain energy when they are close to others, and so they usually enjoy more physical closeness and touching than innies do. Discuss your needs for physicality, because it's one of the keys to maintaining your special connection. Find ways to meet both of your separate needs.

Romance signals to innies that they are appreciated. To outies it signals that they are valued. Romantic touches stir good feelings both innies and outies enjoy. Physical intimacy, obviously an important part of romance, includes hugs, kissing, hand holding, playing footsie under the table, snuggling, cuddling, touching, back rubs, and massages. Discuss the intimate activities you each like. List what you would like more of from the suggestions presented below. Each of you can pick from your partner's list. Give your partner what he or she likes at least once during the upcoming week.

- ☐ I would like a foot massage.

- ☐ I would like to give you a massage.

- ☐ I would like to hold hands when we take a walk.

- ☐ I would like to kiss before bed.

- ☐ I would like to cuddle tonight.

- ☐ I would like to make eye contact during the day.

- ☐ I would like a hug or two today.

- ☐ I would like a back scratch.

- ☐ I would like to sit together with our bodies touching when we watch TV tonight.

- ☐ I would like to be greeted with a slow kiss.

- ☐ I would like to be playful and laugh together.

Warming the Heart with Affection

Another important area in relationships is demonstrating warmth and affection. This is similar to but different from the physical attention we discussed above. Warmth and affection are displayed through gift giving, surprises, showering together, washing each other's hair, sprucing up before lovemaking, writing love letters, sending flowers, watching romantic films together, drawing a bath for your loved one, smiling, laughing, and sharing amusement. Oh yes, and flirting.

Most couples forget to flirt after they have known each other for a while. Innies may never have flirted much at all. But it's a fun way to keep the juices flowing. Flirting shows flattery, admiration, appreciation, and desire. Flirting behaviors include meaningful eye contact, touching in an inviting manner, and wearing sexy clothes. Men may lean toward their gal, and women may show their legs or fiddle with their hair. Approaching your spouse in a playful, laughing, smiling, and lively way is also flirty.

Discuss what "heart warmers" you and your partner like and do a couple for your sweetie during the next few days. And try flirting. You'll probably notice that warmth, affection, and maybe even sparks between you increase.

The Nitty-Gritty: Sex

We recommend that you lie in bed together and read books on sexuality. No, not really—we're just kidding. Let's now get down to the nitty-gritty.

People vary in their comfort levels about discussing sex, partly because discussing sexual feelings requires lowering one's shields. So decide how to discuss the topic if it's uncomfortable—talking in the dark, writing notes to each other, or chatting for five minutes at a time, for example. Remember that your partner trusts you to handle this information gently, so don't trample on any intimate thoughts or feelings he or she reveals. Stay open and understanding, keeping in mind that most sexual tastes are not right or wrong, and that you both need to be comfortable with your lovemaking.

Despite the feelings of embarrassment, it's good for both innies and outies to let their partners know what lights their fire. Partners give each other a gift of love when they reveal their inner selves. Think about the qualities that make sexual experiences satisfying to you. Talk over what you each prefer—your likes and dislikes. As you listen, intercept any defensiveness you feel. If your partner wants a change or suggests trying something new, don't hear it as criticism. Never make fun of or tease your partner about anything he or she says. Practice discussing these tender topics with sensitivity.

SEX TALK IS NOT SHAMEFUL

Sex is one of those subjects shrouded in misunderstanding and shame. Many of us think a good sex life should come naturally. But satisfying lovemaking takes self-knowledge, good communication, lowering shields, caring, and practice. Healthy sex consists of making choices, checking reactions, respect, attraction, playfulness, maintaining bonds, and expressing love. A good sex life is based on the closeness and intimacy you feel together, not to mention those chemicals! Sex takes time. If you aren't putting time into your love life, then it won't be very rewarding. Make it a priority to cuddle, spend time in bed, retire early, talk about sex more, and occasionally send the kids to their grandparents' and stay in bed all day.

The following questions are meant to prime you for a sexual discussion. Discuss your answers right away, or jot them down and talk about them later when you are relaxed. Share your responses, and listen to your partner's answers. Be positive and specific. Agree to check in every week with each other about how your sex life is going.

- What will make it easier for you to talk about making love?

- What setting do you like best?

- What do you like before and after?

- Where do you like to be touched?

- How do you like to be touched?

- Make a list of your ten favorite turn-ons.

- Write another list of your top ten turnoffs.

- I like it when _____.

- I really like it when _____.

- I would like _____.

Keep in mind that there are many benefits to a healthy sexual relationship. A good sex life predicts a happy marriage. Sex improves your mood and sense of well-being. It reduces feelings of isolation because it improves your feeling of connection. Sex reduces pain, PMS symptoms, and reproductive problems in women. It lessens the risk of heart disease, depression, anxiety, and hostility in both men and women. Finally, sex improves your mental health and increases that crucial oxytocin in both you and your partner.

KEEPING LOVE ALIVE: SENSORY SEDUCTION

Your sexual flames are fanned when you turn your senses up. Chemicals are released by heightening your senses and building up sexual anticipation. We often wonder if, in the olden days, the slow process of courting, which was affectionately referred to as "sparking," created a more intense chemical bond. Attraction led to hand holding and talking for quite a while before the couple moved on to a kiss. Inching toward lovemaking would certainly bump up the excitement. Today, with such pressure for instant sexual intimacy, it's easy to see why love peaks and quickly fades. Plan some ways to engage all of your senses by seducing each other, thereby creating a richer emotional and sexual bond.

Sight

Staring into each other's baby blues, browns, and hazels increases your erotic experience. Gaze at each other's lips, brows, and cheeks if eye contact begins to feel too intense. On the other hand, keeping your eyes closed or wearing a blindfold during foreplay increases the release of chemicals related to anticipation, since you don't know what is about to happen.

Disrobing slowly also heightens visual stimulation and amplifies anticipation. Watching each other in the mirror is another way to increase your arousal.

Touch

Touch actually heightens your other senses, such as your vision. Touch releases good-feeling endorphins. Massage each other and vary your touch from light to heavy. Some men enjoy a firmer touch, but not all do, so discuss your preferences. Light tickling can also increase your orgasm. Try gliding your hands over your partner's naked body, hovering just above the skin—not quite touching. The heat and anticipation is arousing.

Scent

Since smells travel quickly to the brain's memory centers, they are very powerful. Smells ignite emotions and arousal. Wear a special scent when you make love (think outside the box—vanilla, grapefruit, chocolate, and so on) and soon you will both associate the aroma with being turned on. Smells spark old memories—the scent of pine may remind you both of a weekend getaway to the woods and the smell of the sea may bring back your honeymoon. Smell each other's hair when you are making love—when you sniff it later it will remind you of your encounter.

Sound

Why not approach your lover and speak in an Italian accent like John Cleese did in the film *A Fish Called Wanda*? It worked for Jamie Lee Curtis's character, who was reduced to quivering Jell-O when Cleese serenaded her in Italian, his voice dripping with spaghetti sauce. Make a sensual soundtrack. Rent the film *Ten* and see how they used the music from *Bolero*. Listen to your own breathing while making love. Matching your breathing with your partner increases your sexual tension. Sharing MP3 earbuds can be very exciting to some couples.

Whispering sweet nothings like "You're great, that feels good, faster, slower, lower, right there, yes, softer" amplifies arousal. Lie in the dark and share made-up fantasy sex encounters. Read erotic books to each other. Talking dirty can embarrass some, especially innies, and reduce sexual feelings. However, listening to a stranger telling an erotic story from an audiobook or downloaded from the Internet is less personal and can be sexier, since it takes the focus off the innie.

Light

Orange, red, pink, and burnt umber all create a warm glow. Candlelight, firelight, and tinted lightbulbs in pink or orange make everyone look better.

Taste

Dip plump strawberries into chocolate and feed each other bites. Lick whipped cream off of each other's bodies. Kiss passionately for several minutes, and really get into the experience. Slowly nibble and kiss various areas of each other's bodies. While kissing, pass a Lifesaver or other hard candy back and forth between your mouths.

Sixth Sense

We mention this last "sense" more for fun than accuracy. Prime your sixth sense. Pick a certain time of day to transmit sexual fantasies to your partner. The next day your partner sends them to you. Check in with each other. Did any messages get through to you? During lovemaking, see if you can guess what your partner desires. Close your eyes and imagine what your partner was thinking and feeling during sex. Later, tell him or her what you imagined. During a romantic dinner, recall a sexual encounter you and your partner shared and see if your spouse can guess which time you are thinking about.

LUBRICATING THE LIBIDO

Wooing and wowing your lover, as we have discussed, are about expressing yourself and expressing love. A passionate connection is made by creating intimacy, sharing memories, and acknowledging each other. Romance is the expression of love. Talking over dinner, making dates, and easing into lovemaking heighten the heat and anticipation.

Introverts are usually reluctant to initiate sexual encounters. Generally, they like a gentler and slower arousal pace, since they need to shift into the mood. Because innies aren't as focused on their external bodies, they may need some time to ease into relaxation. Their outie partner may need to remind him- or herself to slow down and enjoy the anticipation. A hot bath, candles, kissing, eye contact, undressing by candlelight, and music relaxes the introvert's body. Watching a movie or reading a book, whispering, and touching helps an introvert to refocus and wind down his or her busy mind. However, occasionally an innie might do something playful and exciting to turn his or her partner on. Find an innie way to be spontaneous, perhaps focusing on your partner's senses. Sprinkle rose petals into the bedroom, put on some sexy sleep-wear, or invite your partner to hop into an aromatic tub and then meet you in bed.

Extroverts may be ready for love much faster than introverts. They are usually more verbal and their senses are ignited easier. Innies can appreciate outies' efforts to slow the pace when they remember that it's harder for outies to cool their jets. However, distractions need to be kept to a minimum because outies' attention can easily be captured by something else. They may need to refocus if the dog jumps on the bed. Outies enjoy hearing that they are loved and appreciated; they may feel rejected and be hurt more easily than innies might imagine.

GENDER DIFFERENCES

Of course, today we have irrefutable evidence that men and women do have some variations in their brains and bodies. Some of these creep into relationships. None of the research findings is a big surprise. For instance, men really do have chemicals that knock them out immediately after lovemaking. Guys' sexual arousal is stimulated visually. Women need to feel more emotionally connected before they feel like making love.

But here's an interesting bit of research you may not know about. It's the sexual power of helpful hubbies. Researchers have found that men who help out with the household chores have better sex lives, better health, and better marriages (Wolf 1997). Women interpret the help as increasing closeness and partnership. (If you're a man, you may want to take out that trash before reading on.) Studies also show that men consistently overestimate the amount of housework they do. So divvy up the duties and, for some extra zing, try doing them in the nude.

Movies & Books to Spark the Mood

Listed below are some of our favorite romantic movies. Rent one and then sit back, relax, and revel in romance.

- *Somewhere in Time*
- *Dirty Dancing*
- *From Here to Eternity*
- *Charade*

- *Notting Hill*
- *When Harry Met Sally*
- *Bull Durham*
- *Flashdance*
- *Splendor in the Grass*
- *Sleepless in Seattle*
- *Love Actually*

Some erotic books that you might like to read together include the following:

- *Little Birds*, Anais Nin
- *Lady Chatterley's Lover*, D. H. Lawrence
- *Tropic of Cancer*, Henry Miller
- *Yellow Silk*, Lily Pond and Richard Russo
- *The Art of Kissing*, William Cane

You probably have your own list of favorite romantic books and films. Send it to us via e-mail at mikelaney@comcast.net and we will add it to the list on our Web site at www.hiddengifts.net. ♡

7
---

regaining balance
& recharging
boosting batteries

"Well-being is attained little by little, and it is no little thing itself."
—Zeno of Citium

We can't get much done in life without energy. It's a vital force we all need. Energy spikes and dips just like blood pressure. Its constant shifting makes it a confusing force, so it's hard to pin down. Nevertheless, both innies and outies need to be aware of their fluctuating energy levels. As we discussed in chapter 2, we are all born with a set point firmly planted on the energy continuum. We function best when we are in our comfort zone, the area near our set point. If we move outside our comfort zone for too long, we will become stressed. Then we are spending too much energy, or we aren't able to create new energy. High stress levels drain our batteries. Even so, sometimes we try to ignore our depleted batteries and push on. Picture yourself driving a car while mashing on the brake and gas pedal simultaneously—your wheels would just spin, with a lot of energy going nowhere.

Innies who are drained take longer to recoup their energy, so it is especially important for them to avoid too much stress and not force themselves to run on empty. Outies have a paradoxical energy conundrum. Stress can actually cause outies to gain too much energy, so they do, do, do—and spin out of control. But even though outies' energy is drained by a lack of stimulation, without rest and relaxation their health can be damaged. Let's look at what happens when we are stressed, and then we'll take a further look at how stress affects both innies and outies.

Impact of Stress on Innies & Outies

Guess what? Stress is a part of life and it affects everyone. We all get out of balance occasionally. Stress is tricky because it's subjective; it's in the eye of the beholder. Each person feels stressed as a result of different experiences. What stresses one person may not bother someone else at all. For instance, outies may appreciate a deadline, since it helps them focus. Innies, on the other hand, don't perform as well under pressure because their process is slower. Begin to notice what pushes your and your partner's stress buttons.

Stress is created from both good and bad events. We all are used to feeling stress when we are faced with a new, unpleasant, boring, or threatening situation. Many people are surprised to find that even good experiences like winning the lottery, getting married, and having a baby push stress buttons. But stress makes life exciting, too. It blasts us out of our ruts, it alerts us to danger, and it points us toward what we really need and want.

VAGAL BRAKE

Because too much stress affects the health of both innies' and outies' bodies and relationships, we all have a vital built-in stress reducer called the "vagal brake," a little-known but very important aspect of our physical well-being. It adjusts our body's reactions to varying levels of stress. The vagal brake turns off the spending (sympathetic) side of the nervous system and turns on the conserving (parasympathetic) side (check out the illustration on page 40). The vagal brake helps us to switch off our emergency system, keeping us from burning out. The vagal brake is triggered by acetylcholine (the neurotransmitter favored by introverts' brains). When calm is needed, it switches on the conserving, "rest and digest" functions (Beauchaine 2001). The mind and body then slow down to evaluate the threat. (Remember, the conserving side of the nervous system is the introvert's dominant system.) Without a responsive vagal brake, people would stay in a constant state of emergency.

In a highly stressful situation, or one that is perceived as threatening, adrenaline is released to power up the flight, fight, or fright side (the spending side, favored by extroverts) of the nervous system. It gives us gallons of fuel so we can prepare to flee, fight, or freeze. Muscles become tense, and heart rate and breathing increase. Adrenaline, a neurotransmitter, is released to allow the person to handle the short-term emergency. Cortisol, a steroid, is released to sustain adrenaline during the crisis. Once some time has passed, the nervous system expects the high stress level to be over, so the "rest and digest," or conserving, side of the nervous system begins to restore our depleted resources.

Innies are dominant on the rest and digest side of the nervous system, which controls the vagus nerve. When an innie is threatened and adrenaline is released, the flight, fight, or fright side of the system causes them to feel antsy or frozen—or both (the brake and gas pedals being applied simultaneously). To most innies, these adrenaline surges are painful and feel like overdoses of caffeine, or like ants crawling under their skin. Some innies may feel antsy and flee the scene. Others will freeze like rabbits caught in headlights. Responding to the adrenaline and cortisol surge from a stressor, they release acetylcholine, and their vagal brake shuts them down. After this process occurs, it takes time for all of the spending chemicals to disperse. And the chemicals that introverts use to recharge take more time to be restored. This is why innies take longer to recover their equilibrium after stress and emergencies.

When an outie feels threatened, adrenaline is released and the fight, flight, or fright system is fired up. Generally, for an outie the experience of an adrenaline rush isn't uncomfortable like it is for an innie; instead, outies usually find it to be enjoyable and exciting. They can even become addicted to it. This explains why some people love to bungee jump, skydive, and perform other daring adventures, doesn't it? Outies tend to travel down the fight-or-flight track—they either become angry or run for the hills. This is why some outies are frequently irritable; like match-sticks, they can be easily sparked. When cortisol is released in an outie, it doesn't activate the vagal brake as quickly, which explains why outies may have trouble calming down and cooling their jets. However, outies, who are already using the spending side of the nervous system, can harm their health if they don't shift to the conserving side occasionally.

SIGNS THAT INNIES ARE STRESSED

- They become frozen, feel frazzled, or want to flee.
- They feel pooped, irritable, worried, and fearful.
- They have trouble falling asleep or waking up.
- They feel overwhelmed and can't think or concentrate.

- They may ruminate, hear critical inner voices, or relive painful experiences.
- They can't make decisions.

SIGNS THAT OUTIES ARE STRESSED

- They feel anxious, tense, and pressed for time.
- They can't stop doing too much; their thoughts race.
- They wake up often during the night or have trouble falling asleep.
- They act too quickly and make poor or impulsive choices.
- They feel drowsy, fidget, or can't sit still.
- They engage in obsessive behaviors such as eating, drinking, shopping, or gambling.

KEEP YOUR ENERGY FLOWING

Energy needs to be usable and available. We usually enjoy and feel more energized when we are doing something we like. Introverts generate energy, "hap hits" (good feelings), and a sense of satisfaction when they focus on their inner reflections. Turning outward requires innies to spend gobs of energy. If they are out in the world too much, they can zone out or feel that they're dragging as their energy drains away. They need a low-stimulation environment where they can recharge their batteries. Extroverts produce energy, hap hits, and feelings of well-being when they are interacting with people, objects, and activities. When they turn inward they start to sag, because without external stimuli their energy isn't generated. To boost their batteries they need to get a move on.

As we have seen, one of the most important aspects of temperament is where we fall on the temperament continuum. As Jung said, we all naturally function better on one side of the temperament energy continuum or the other. In Jungian terms, balance doesn't mean having equal energy on both sides of the continuum. It means hovering around your comfort zone most of the time. When we are stressed out we need to return to our normal comfort zone to recharge. A good way to maintain energy balance is to use your less-dominant side of the nervous system during relaxation, hobbies, and nonwork activities. Partners can remind each other to recharge and regain their energy balance.

Whole Brain Gains & Drains

In this section we are going to discuss whole brain energy. As you recall, the whole brain includes the extrovert's dominant back of the brain and the introvert's dominant front of the brain, with preferences for the right or left hemispheres. If you don't know which is your and your partner's dominant brain hemisphere, look over the list at the end of chapter 2. Because you can increase your brain power when you know your brain better, we suggest that you and your partner read over the descriptions below and discuss which whole brain profile fits you best.

We are using the term "brain energy" to mean two things: mental energy, which is influenced by introverted and extroverted temperaments, and emotional energy, which is created through left- or right-brain dominance. Different conditions cause left- and right-brained innies and outies to either gain or lose mental and emotional energy. These two forms of energy establish how we behave in relationships. In this chapter, you will learn to reduce or "undress" your stress by practicing a few new techniques. You will also understand your partner better when you see how mental and emotional energy influence your relationship.

In the four profiles discussed below, we describe what charges up these people's energy ("gainers") and what sucks their energy ("drainers"). Conditions increasing or decreasing stress are called stressors and "undressers." Finally, we suggest ways to bolster emotional energy.

LEFT-BRAINED EXTROVERTS

Left-brained outies are gifted at organization, coordination, thinking, and compartmentalizing. Their favorite phrases are "This is how to do it," and "People should do . . ."

GAINERS: Left-brained extroverts are the majority in the population. The left hemisphere of the brain is where math and language skills are developed. Its strength is detailed and logical thinking. Mike is a left-brainer. Energizers for him are focusing on his career, feeling competent, taking action, analyzing, directing and leading others, achieving closure, and interacting in a logical, predictable environment. (In other words, these folks tend to be a bit bossy.) The left hemisphere of the brain is dominated by dopamine. Left-brained people usually have more mental energy but less emotional energy than right-brainers.

DRAINERS: Stressors for Mike and other left-brained extroverts are feeling helpless, feeling disorganized, and encountering illogical behavior, incompetence (his own or others'), criticism, unclear expectations, and precipitous action. Like other left-brained extroverts, Mike can experience emotions as being intimidating and irritating. When he's under stress his normally buttoned-down emotions can suddenly surface, and he can become obsessive, demanding, and dictatorial. Although Mike is usually reasonable, when stressed he may take things personally, feel unappreciated, and become defensive. When his feelings erupt he might overreact to his own and others' emotions. He feels out of control and vulnerable, like a stranger in a strange land.

STRESSORS: Emotions are a major stressor for left-brained outies. Other people's emotionality, including their spouse's, may cause extroverts to feel that their own values are being disregarded. When they feel remorse over their own reactions, they become flooded with emotions. Since they have trouble regulating and expressing their feelings, they can show outbursts of anger and may become inflexible, domineering, and withdrawn. When under extreme stress, they may think others don't like them. In the case of chronic stress, feelings may be expressed through illnesses.

UNDRESS YOUR STRESS: Left-brained outies' stress is reduced when they calm their emotions, are physically active, or refocus their energy. They feel more in control if they can see that they aren't helpless and that they have choices. They can regain their balance by recognizing their feelings and talking to a trusted partner or friend about their emotions. They can learn to calm their emotions and see them as helpful information. Developing emotional awareness and using their natural talent for thinking helps their social interactions. Exercise works off their anxiety. Balancing doing with being can increase their energy, lessen their dependence on adrenaline, and expand their lives.

BUILD ENERGY: Left-brained extroverts can learn to accept the irrational side of humans, to set their own limits, and to value their intimate relationships. Here are a few right-brain-oriented exercises that left-brained outies can do to provide more balance in their relationships:

- Get to know your spouse better. In a relaxed setting, ask your partner about his or her thoughts and feelings. Notice your partner's emotions and body language. Adjust your responses to mirror and reflect your partner's reactions.

- When taking action, consider how your partner and children will be affected. Step into your partner's and your children's shoes. Ask your partner for his or her viewpoint before you take action.

LEFT-BRAINED INTROVERTS

Left-brained introverts are consistent, principled, and good at analysis, with a tendency to classify and categorize. Their favorite comments are "This is why," and "It does that because . . ."

GAINERS: Introverted thinking folks typically focus on facts, steps in a process, and their own perceptions. Since the left brain is dopamine dominant, left-brained innies usually have more physical energy than right-brained innies. They don't find word retrieval quite as challenging either because language centers are on the left side. For example, Mark, an objective, dispassionate observer who enjoys detailed analysis, sees criticism and disagreement as constructive, but he unknowingly offends others with his objective critiques. He may appear unfeeling, disinterested, distant, and even arrogant. He is fueled when he can work on a project independently, intensely, and as long as he believes is necessary to achieve tangible results. He likes his expertise respected, his contributions appreciated and considered.

DRAINERS: Mark feels constricted by strict rules and regulations. When he feels responsible and dependent on the work of people he believes are incompetent, illogical, unjust, or unfair, this frustrates and stifles his efforts. Mark's batteries will drain quickly if he experiences strong emotions, too little time alone, too much extroverting, or supervising too many people. He needs to set limits so that he doesn't have too much socializing time.

STRESSORS: Any strong emotions are triggers for left-brained innies. Attempting to keep a lid on their own emotions creates stress. When pressured they may feel the need to prove their perceptions are right. Time pressures and being evaluated are big stressors to these innies. They tend to take things personally and interpret others' actions as slights against them. They can begin to feel alienated from others. They need both emotional support and time alone.

UNDRESS YOUR STRESS: When left-brained innies realize that they are sensitive to others' reactions they will handle their stress better. Reducing their perception that others are against them decreases their sense of isolation. Building in alone time to recover and regroup improves their outlook. They can secure a better balance when they realize that everyone's life is stressful, and that they aren't doing anything wrong to produce the stress. Awareness increases a left-brained innie's confidence to deal with normal stresses and strains.

BUILD ENERGY: Left-brained innies can learn that human behavior is logical and explainable. Emotions can be helpful and even bring them closer to others. They can learn to accept that they aren't always in control. By becoming less sensitive and worried about their social performance, they can enjoy socializing more. Here are a few suggestions that left-brained introverts can use to improve their relationships and achieve better balance in their lives:

- Think of something you deeply value about your partner and, in a private setting, discuss this with him or her. Let your loved one know how much he or she improves your life.

- The next time you have a conflict with your spouse or someone important to you, ask yourself the following questions: What is most important to me about this relationship? Do I have to be right? Could I let go of something? How would I feel if I compromised? Discuss your thoughts and feelings openly and honestly with your partner.

RIGHT-BRAINED EXTROVERTS

Right-brained outies are considerate, accommodating, and affirming. They tend to say things like "This is what we need," and "We do it this way . . ."

GAINERS: Right-brained extroverts feel energized when they are in a supportive and sociable environment where they are in charge of their responsibilities. For example, Megan, a right-brained outie, likes to be appreciated for her contributions and is enthused when she feels in tune with and connected to her partner. She uses less energy when she knows others around her maintain open and honest communication.

DRAINERS: Megan is drained by divisive hassles, conflicts, unco-operative people, and criticism. Sudden changes and demanding time pressures suck her energy. Her fuel is gobbled up when she must relate in impersonal ways or when her integrity and values are violated.

STRESSORS: When relationships lack trust, have lots of conflict, or require conformity, right-brained outies feel stressed. They may feel excessively criticized and their logic may become convoluted. They often think that finding answers will relieve their anxiety. They sometimes begin to rely on magical thinking, turning to practices such as astrology and seeking other cosmic hints to guide their decisions.

UNDRESS YOUR STRESS: Right-brained outies can reduce their stress by spending some time in solitude, talking with their partner, writing in a journal, or beginning a new project. They also find it helpful to relate to other outies with similar values. Discussing the issues causing the stress will help reduce feelings of tension.

BUILD ENERGY: Right-brained outies can lessen their need for harmony, learn to temper their reactions to adversity, and begin to trust their own logical thinking. To balance their right-brain tendencies with left-brain thinking, right-brained outies can try the following suggestions:

- Ask your partner to discuss a disagreement between you. Talk about your feelings and ask for your partner's. Reframe the disagreement as a problem-solving challenge.

- Set a goal to finish a task like cleaning out the garage. Break the job into small steps and jot them down. You and your partner can each select the jobs you each prefer. Cross off the tasks as you complete them. Enjoy working with your partner, engaging in the physical activity, and accomplishing small steps toward your goal. Afterward, celebrate by doing something fun.

RIGHT-BRAINED INTROVERTS

Right-brained introverts have strong values and they want harmony, clarification, congruency, and reconciliation. Statements you hear from them might include "This is important," and "I (or you) do your best when . . ."

GAINERS: Marti is a right-brained introvert. She is energized by work that is aligned with her values. She enjoys helping and affirming others. She likes to be in an open, cooperative, and congenial atmosphere. She has more energy when what is important to her is appreciated and valued. When her expertise and contributions are seen and acknowledged she can put herself out in the world without burning so much fuel. Her working process takes time, so she has better results and enjoys her work more when she is working under relaxed deadlines.

DRAINERS: When Marti has multiple demands, roles, and projects going on at the same time she may become drained and scattered. Rigid, pressured, and hostile environments diminish her energy. Dealing with people who confront, control, and demand wears her out. She feels debilitated if she must do something she finds unacceptable.

STRESSORS: Distrust, negativity, and disappointment stress right-brained introverts. Since their relationships are important to them they become stressed if those connections are threatened. When others violate their values they can find it very upsetting. Marti can lose her footing if her perception of her own competence is shaken.

UNDRESS YOUR STRESS: Right-brained innies can increase their ability to cope with disappointments and hostility. Noticing feelings, writing about them, or discussing their emotions helps them sift and sort their reactions. When their feelings are validated and processed they can move on. However, if left-brained partners try to reason with them without acknowledging their spouse's right-brained feelings, it only makes things worse. Since right-brained innies may depend upon what others believe, it can be helpful for them to develop assertiveness skills. When they recognize their own talents and abilities, they can use their gifts to develop a better world, as long as they remember that it's a long-term project.

BUILD ENERGY: Right-brained introverts can learn that it's okay for them to show personal strengths in the outside world. When right-brained innies learn to count on their own skills and abilities they are better able to extrovert without feeling drained of energy. However, they need to learn to recognize and protect themselves from people who don't have the best intentions. Redirecting energy away from destructive relationships and unfulfilling jobs and refocusing their strengths toward their own interests will improve their lives, allowing them to pursue their own desires and needs. Right-brained introverts can use the following suggestions to balance their energy:

- Guess people's motivations. Notice negative and positive traits. Ask yourself, Are they more thinking or feeling people? Do they want to be right, or do they try to be cooperative? Stay in touch with the emotional signals you are receiving.

- When your partner talks to you about a problem, see if you can listen for the major thinking points he or she is discussing. The feelings your partner expresses may be quite clear to you; instead, focus on the factual, rational aspects of the problem. Suggest a few practical solutions.

Balancing on the Energy Tightrope

Expand your ability to balance your emotional energy with your mental energy by learning various techniques to subdue stress and renew your energy. It is like sliding your feet along a tightrope, carefully balancing so you won't fall off. Practice as many stress "undressers" as you can; some will work better than others, and some may work well one day and poorly another. We all have to move outside our comfort zones at times, so it's an ongoing task to negotiate that tightrope and create an energy balance that's just right for you. Persistence, flexibility, and practice are the keys.

REGAINING EMOTIONAL BALANCE

In the next few days, when you are confronted with a stressor, stop for a moment and tune in to your emotional reaction. In the context of brain research, motion means moving our body, moving our thoughts (thinking), or moving our feelings (emotions). Paying attention and processing our emotions "moves" or integrates the five layers of the brain. In the pages that follow, we discuss how to reduce stressors and learn to balance emotions.

Often emotions are sparked by a particular event or action. When you experience an uncomfortable feeling, think over the questions below and write down your thoughts. Writing is another way to slow impulsivity and it helps you to integrate your thoughts and feelings. Please also discuss these questions with your partner—it will increase your intimacy.

- What bothered you most about what happened?
- What was the exact situation that caused the stress?
- What was your initial reaction?
- What feelings did you have? Thoughts?
- What solutions can you choose to "undress" the emotions underneath your stress?

Anger

People are born with individual thresholds for all emotions, including fear, shame, guilt, and anger. As we mentioned earlier, some folks are like matchsticks that go up in flames easily; others hold on to anger for long periods of time and finally explode. Men and women often handle anger differently. Some men yell; others become passive-aggressive, and withdraw. They may "accidentally" forget the milk their partner asked them to bring home from the store. Some women pitch fits, some cry, and still others shop to express their anger. Each of us has our own ways of showing anger. Notice how you and your partner tend to show anger, and discuss it.

Anger can be a valuable signal that a boundary needs to be set. When our threat system is triggered we feel either anger or fear—sometimes both. Fear is often covered up by anger.

Learning to cool down is essential, because anger releases adrenaline and other chemicals that aren't good for the body. Mentally replaying what you are angry about only increases your chemical output. To calm down, take a moment to breathe deeply and stop thinking about what is bugging you. Give yourself a time-out if you can't calm down right away, and count to ten. If that doesn't do it, count until you reach one hundred. By the time you're done, you'll probably feel a bit calmer.

Exercise is a good way to work off steam. You can also release some steam by interrupting your internal critic's angry voice mails or e-mails that you are receiving. Distractions can help you stop replaying upsetting situations. Watching some TV or reading an engrossing book might help to keep your mind focused on something other than the cause of your anger while your body relaxes. Breathe in and out and tell yourself that you are okay. Step back and see the humor in the situation. Later, when you're less governed by your anger, you might even recall times when you have had fun with the annoying person. Move your mind on and plan for a future fun event. If your anger is hard to let go of, try two anger-reducing exercises that Marti's clients have found useful. Write down what has happened and then burn the page in the fireplace. Or write the name of the person you're mad at on the bottom of your shoe and then "step on" that person all day. These techniques will release a lot of anger in a nonconfrontational way.

After some time has passed, you can reflect on the situation. Was someone angry at you? Did that set off your anger? Did it trigger a note from an old familiar tune? In other words, did someone tell you something like "You are selfish," echoing similar messages you had received as a child? If so, you may have had a volcanic eruption of anger because hearing that dreaded pronouncement triggered shame and fear that have lain dormant inside you for years. (If you felt criticized because your parents thought you were self-absorbed, you may feel comforted to know that critical comments often say more about the speaker than about you, and that we are all selfish at times.)

Here is a list of steps you might try with your partner:

1. State your observations about the problem. "The roof is leaking. You agreed to call a repair person two weeks ago, and so far nothing has happened."

2. Say what you think: "The longer the roof goes unrepaired, the more likely it is that rain could damage the house."

3. State your feelings: "I am scared and frustrated that the roof isn't fixed. I'm disappointed that you haven't followed through by calling the roofers."

4. Say what you want: "I want the roof fixed by next weekend. If you can't get it done, I'll have someone come and fix it the following Monday. And I would like you to pick one of my chores to do this week."

Anxiety

Anxiety is a free-floating fear about the future. If you're feeling anxious, then something you may not be aware of is triggering your fright, flight, or fight system. Outies tend to have more anxiety since they are using the sympathetic side of the nervous system. Anxiety can heighten our awareness of possible danger. Pay attention to the butterflies in your tummy, shallow breathing, sweaty and clammy palms, pounding heart, and tense muscles. Notice what thoughts preceded the anxiety. Is the thing you're worried about really a serious threat? Perhaps you don't have your work-related presentation ready, but it's not a life-threatening situation. Remind yourself that anxiety is just a normal body reaction. Shift your thoughts away from worry or anticipating a negative outcome. Tell yourself it will be okay. Breathe. Get some vigorous exercise. Think over what's bothering you, discuss your anxiety with your partner, and figure out what you can do to deal with the problem. Remind yourself that you can't always anticipate what will happen.

Also, notice whether you are fantasizing about a positive, or negative, outcome. Has it developed into an expectation? You may be expecting something bad to happen—or something good. Don't get ahead of yourself. Stay in the moment, and remind yourself that you are okay right now. Maybe it will help to discuss with your partner the feelings you are experiencing right now.

Depression

We all feel down in the dumps occasionally. It's a natural reaction to disappointment and loss. Innies tend to have more depression, since they utilize the parasympathetic side of the nervous system. This is why their outie partners, who are typically good at taking action, can help them lift their depression. If you are depressed for quite a while, you will need to take physical action. Go for a walk around the block. Moving the body is a depression lifter. Write. Go to a sad movie and cry to release your feelings. Get some rest. Talk to an understanding friend. Get more sunlight or use a sun lamp on dark winter days. Always remind yourself (or have your partner remind you) that low moods pass. If, however, your depression continues, please see a doctor and consider medication. Antidepressants and talk therapy are very effective for depression.

Shame and Guilt

In children, a dash of shame can be constructive; when parents say no to a toddler, it triggers the vagal brake to slow the child down. It's how we become socialized. However, children are often shamed too much (today, sometimes too little). Shaming results in deep-seated feelings of being bad. Adults who have been shamed a lot feel helpless to do anything about feeling bad. They experience a sinking feeling and want to hide, wishing that the floor would open up and swallow them. Shame is a tricky feeling because many times people are swimming in shame, yet they aren't aware of it. They just want to retreat or escape.

Outies experience more shame because it is a reaction to the disapproval of others. It switches off the good-feeling, spending side of their nervous system and causes them to slow down, a feeling they don't like. Innies are accustomed to switching to the conserving side of the nervous system and they don't miss the spending side as much. For this reason, many innies aren't as damaged by shame.

Shame is often disguised as anger. If you feel angry and wish you could disappear, allow yourself to calm down and ponder what triggered the shame. It's likely that you were wanting something or someone's approval.

Guilt is a feeling that you have done something wrong, either by thought or by deed. It is meant to motivate people to repair hurt feelings or misdeeds. Many innies who are sensitive to others feel guilty when they have *thought* something but didn't really *do* anything wrong. Everyone should feel guilty at times, since we all do the wrong thing occasionally;

people who don't feel guilt are usually classified as sociopaths (individuals who don't have a conscience). If you feel guilty, think about what you may have done wrong. If you did harm someone, apologize. If not, let it go.

EMOTIONAL FIRST-AID KIT

It's easier to face emotional stress if you have prepared an emotional first-aid kit. Fill it with good friends who listen—people who listen to you without automatically giving advice when you talk about difficult feelings such as grief, helplessness, vulnerability, and fear. Stick in some self-acceptance—don't blame yourself when things go wrong. Calm yourself if you are anxious, and boot yourself out the door if you are depressed. Then add a big helping of faith in the goodness of trustworthy people. Even in dire circumstances, stay optimistic about humanity.

REGAINING MENTAL ENERGY BALANCE

Here are some suggestions that you and your partner can use to regain balance and restore mental energy. Pick one to practice and see if it helps. Some take a few tries; the brain learns by trial and error. There is no one right way for everyone.

Sit Still

Not doing isn't the same as doing nothing. Find stillness in everyday life by sitting and being fully present, in that one moment, wherever you may be. It can be anywhere, even in a bathroom. Couples who sit together quietly can be very intimate.

Relax Your Mind

Meditation refreshes your mind, clarifies thoughts and feelings, and recharges your energy, whether you are an innie or an outie. Start the day with ten minutes of meditation. Sit in a comfortable position with your back straight, and breathe in and out while repeating a word like "peace," or some other word with meaning. If your mind wanders, gently guide it back. After a while you will feel more at peace—you are okay right now, just the way you are. Other ways of relaxing the mind include taking time-outs to unwind, humming, listening to a relaxation tape, moving the body to music, catching a relaxing TV show, reading, writing, looking at nature, and thinking pleasant thoughts.

Gratitude

Start the day by reading something inspirational. End your day by writing in a journal three things you are grateful for. Gratitude is the opposite of envy and it is a direct route to happiness and health.

Sweet Retreat

Stake out a place of your own. Create a place of calm, harmony, and rest. It can be a closet, a nook of the attic, or a corner in the basement. If you don't have any extra space, put a chair in the corner of your bedroom, on the porch, or in a breakfast nook. All you need is some warm light, relaxing colors, meaningful pictures, throw pillows, scented candles, and a few of your favorite books. It's a place for kicking back, reading, meditating, reflecting, staring at your navel, or having some tea. Keep it free of clutter, and make it calm, clean, and inviting. Protect your space from invaders; ask that you not be interrupted unless a family member loses a limb or a fire breaks out. Today we are all bombarded by noise, making us feel discombobulated and unsettled. Remember that the word "noisy" comes from the Latin term for nausea or seasickness. Establish a family or couple quiet time. Kids and parents need to be reminded that it's good to be quiet sometimes.

Internal Chatter

You may or may not be conscious of the fact that internal self-talk is quietly or not-so-quietly going on in your noodle. Innies have a lot of noisy chattering in their heads. Internal talking is a valuable ability because it inhibits impulsive action. But it can also be crippling, if the chatter is negative and reinforces critical beliefs about ourselves. Such internal tapes drain our energy and influence how we respond to situations. You can learn to identify, challenge, and change negative self-talk. You can develop positive self-talk, which stokes your energy and helps you to manage stress. Erase critical self-talk and rerecord kinder commentary in your head, such as "I am all right. I will get better at this."

Just Say No

You have a right to say no. Learning how to say no to requests is an essential life skill. Innies and right-brained people are often reluctant to say no. If you haven't decided just yet how to respond to a request, tell the person that you need to take some time before you answer. Then separate the request from the person, and decide on your response and rehearse your answer. Acknowledge the importance of the request when you respond. You might say something like "Thanks for wanting to include us, but I'm afraid we can't make it." If you want to, make a counteroffer, such as "We'd love to be included next time. Thanks for the invite."

Divide & Conquer

Energy is drained when you feel overwhelmed, especially for innies. Outies may feel overwhelmed and not know it. To-do lists will help you both. Make a list of what you need to do. Prioritize your top three tasks for the day. Write your top priorities in red and the next six tasks in another color, like purple. Pick a third color, perhaps blue, for the rest of your list. Break your top priorities into smaller action steps. Cross them off with a green pen as you complete each task. If you accomplish any other tasks not on your list, write them down and cross them off. This will give you a great feeling of accomplishment. Congratulate yourself for whatever you finished, and don't attack yourself for not completing tasks. They'll just go on tomorrow's list. ♡

8

the more things change . . .
adjusting to life

"We must always change, renew, rejuvenate ourselves;
otherwise we harden." —Johann Wolfgang von Goethe

Life is like a stretched-out slinky; it is full of continuous cycles of change. Paradoxically, as the well-known cliché goes, "the more things change, the more they stay the same." This is because life, at its essence, is made up of changing patterns. Yet humans usually fight change instead of accepting and adjusting to natural shifts in life.

Going with Life's Flows

Recently, we asked a group of therapists how many of them were experiencing significant changes in their life. Every hand went up. So we know that change is common to everyone. And although each change may seem very different, changes follow similar patterns, which couples can learn to recognize. We all wander down life's path constantly facing transitions. Our lives are a series of big changes: marriage, births, illnesses, parents aging, pets dying or getting lost, promotions, demotions, new stages of marriage, new jobs, new homes, children entering new stages, children leaving home, financial changes, and friends dying or moving away. Every day we are also faced with small changes. The cat hurls a fur ball, you get a surprise invitation, a spot wrecks your favorite shirt, you discover that you hate the movie you chose, your friend cancels lunch, and so it goes, on and on. These big and small changes are all challenging to deal with. But change gets even trickier when we believe widespread myths about it.

MYTHS ABOUT CHANGE

The myths about change listed below often become stumbling blocks for us, keeping us from accepting and adjusting to change. Without change we stagnate. However, if you update your view of change, you will be helping yourself and your partner learn to flow with life. Discuss your reactions to the myths listed below with your partner.

MYTH: Change means sacrifice.

TRUTH: Change means loss and adding new behaviors, ideas, and choices.

MYTH: Change means trying harder and doing more.

TRUTH: Change usually offers us the opportunity to do things in a different and sometimes easier way.

MYTH: Change takes a long time.

TRUTH:	Some changes are slow and others happen as quickly as a snap of your fingers.
MYTH:	Change means giving in or becoming who my spouse wants me to be.
TRUTH:	Accepting or embracing change means making a commitment.

Handling Changes

How do innies and outies tend to handle change? Even if changes are positive they can prove to be troublesome for innie and outie couples. Change upsets the applecart. The Chinese symbol for the word "crisis" (a quick change) is composed of two signs meaning "opportunity" and "danger." Changes affect innies' and outies' energy levels, throwing them out of their comfort zone. This constant lack of stability is like a flower-pot filled with sand—energy drains right out of it. Adapting to change takes energy, and more so for innies, who often become tired and need to withdraw. For outies, change gives them lots to focus on and they may spring into action; at times, outies may not even realize they are stressed out by changes since they feel peppy. Change also affects the actions innies and outies take. Innies may make incomplete decisions if they are pushed. Outies, on the other hand, may need to slow down to reflect and consider all the options before taking action.

Relationship pressures build up during change, causing innies and outies to become stressed. If this pressure lasts too long it turns into chronic stress. (See chapter 7 for a discussion of how to manage stress.) Of course, it's best if couples lend each other a hand, encourage each other, and learn to go with the flow. Innies and outies can join hands and support each other during changes and transitions. Coping with a major life transition like children leaving home is less disruptive when faced together. Couples can encourage each other during both major transitions and everyday minor annoyances or stresses.

Three Life Secrets

Let's stand back and take a larger gander at life. The b-i-g picture. Transitions draw our attention to basic secrets about life. One secret is that everything in nature grows. The second is that reality is a bitch. And the last is that we should wake up and smell the coffee. If you want to increase your marital intimacy and create a more meaningful life, read more about the life secrets below.

EVERYTHING GROWS

As we mentioned in chapter 2, we are born half-baked. At birth, our brains are disorganized, with only a few basic regions wired into pathways. Most of the acetylcholine pathways that innies travel and all of the dopamine pathways outies travel are prewired. This allows us to make basic, simple responses to the world. It takes almost thirty years for us to wire pathways into networks throughout the brain. Networks link regions from the lizard brain all the way up to the CEO frontal area of the brain. This arrangement provides an incredible choice of responses from the simple to the complex, allowing us to gain maturity (defined as the ability to respond to life with sophisticated coping skills).

Surprisingly, some folks resist growing. They find the idea of psychological development or self-growth to be threatening. They say, "I'm fine as I am," "Take me as I am," or "I like to stay the same; I don't want to become a stranger to myself." These responses are based on fear. Some people fear the responsibility of growing up; others may fear that they'll discover that something is fundamentally wrong with them, or that they'll fail if they do try to change. This is a very limiting way to deal with life, because the person will never fully develop. It's like remaining a rosebud all your life—never blossoming into a luscious, ripe rose. Resisting growth kills relationships. Couples who don't grow together dry up, wither, and fall off the relationship vine.

Innies and outies choosing to grow and develop will reap personal, relationship, and career rewards. Not surprisingly, the growth work that innies and outies must do differs. Innies, who may have trouble showing their inner resources, often feel satisfied figuring something out for themselves and don't take the next step, in which they would put their work out into the world. Sharing their work, ideas, and solutions is taking a growth step for these innies. Outies often get into reacting loops, running around and around in the same circle. A growth step for them would be to suspend action in order to develop more complex responses. Without the ability to grow we can't learn from our experiences and develop better coping and relationship skills.

REALITY IS A BITCH

The second secret to life is that reality is a bitch. It's true. Seeing life as it really is can be very painful at times. However, if you don't face reality, you'll be in worse shape. And, to make matters worse, our brains make it difficult for us to see reality. Believe it or not, we live in the interior world of our own brain, which may not mirror what's actually going on around us. Amazing, isn't it? But it does explain a lot about puzzling human behavior. Why do we have such difficulty seeing reality? In any given situation, our brains quickly assess the environment and try to make sense of what's happening based on our former experiences. We are always attempting to piece the world together, and we don't always get it right. When twenty witnesses to an event are asked to describe what they saw, officials hear twenty different stories. For example, a very observant and intelligent client of Marti's once saw her take a glass out of her office. She took it into a private area and closed the door. Because of experiences in the client's childhood, he assumed that she was bringing a drink to someone in the room on the other side of the door. When Marti came back with a fresh glass of water and set it on the table beside him, he never registered it. It didn't fit his prewired story, which told him that she was taking the drink to someone in the other room.

More poignantly, some people resist the pain of reality, especially if they have lived through trauma. They have defense mechanisms that give them good-feeling endorphins for staying dissociated. With dissociation, the associations that connect all of the stored bits of experience throughout the brain are disconnected. Life for someone who is in a state of dissociation is a fragmented puzzle. The entire picture of reality is broken up into hundreds of fragments, and they can't see the entire picture. This keeps reality at bay. Similarly, innies can avoid reality by getting stuck in their own interior worlds, so they forget to get feedback, practice in the real world, or test their ideas. Conversely, outies make snap judgments about what's real. They may decide on actions without listening to other views or integrating input based on changes in reality.

WAKE UP

The third secret in life is to wake up. Even with lots of effort, our brains primarily function unconsciously. Our heart is beating, our feet are walking, our stomach is digesting lunch, and our unconscious is processing gobs of information. All of these and even more functions are out of our awareness. Switching off our automatic pilot and becoming conscious takes energy and practice. People who are living on automatic pilot are driven and motivated by unconscious expectations. They rush from place to place without stepping back and wondering if what they are doing is even important to them. They are like rats on wheels. Real life always surprises them. They make comments like "I wasn't expecting that," and "It didn't turn out the way I expected." It takes practice to stay alert to the present. What are you doing right now? You're reading, of course. But you may be looking at the words on the page and thinking about picking up your cleaning. If you don't really attend to what you are doing in the present moment, if you are constantly multitasking, it usually means you are living an unconscious life. You may not be living based on your conscious needs and wants.

Outies are prone to living on automatic pilot because their greased-lightning processing ignores unconscious input. They move now and think later. They aren't integrating their brain stacks. "That's too deep, complex, or confusing for me," they say. They want momentary stimulation. They move away from further exploration, skimming the surface of life without digging deeper into the underlying meanings. Innies, on the other hand, may not realize that they must take time to process all they have absorbed both unconsciously and consciously. "I'm not sure what I think or feel yet," they might say. For both innies and outies, consciousness is a simple, direct route to vitality and wisdom. This means consciously choosing the direction and quality of your life and your relationships. Consciousness, or waking up, is like sliding into the driver's seat and steering your own life. Without consciousness you are either asleep at the wheel or, even worse, running along beside your life.

The Gift of the Present Moment

We can spend our whole lives being robots, living without consciousness. Or we can practice becoming more conscious and present. You and your partner can encourage each other to wake up and grab the steering wheel of your life. Try these steps, which will help you learn to slow down and enter the present. You can do them by yourself or with your partner, and you can practice them together.

1. Pause. Occasionally stop and smell the petunias. See? Were you expecting roses? Notice things you don't usually focus on—flowers, birds, the sidewalk, car sounds, rain on your face, or the smell of smoke from a chimney on a fall day. Take a walk together after dinner and hold hands. Take turns pointing out bits of reality.

2. Stop. Find a bench in a beautiful, soothing spot and sit together. Notice your breathing. Relax and notice the present moment. What is happening in your body? How are you feeling? What are you thinking? Scan your body for emotions and thoughts. After a while, share your experience with your partner.

3. Quiet your mind. Light some vanilla candles and sit together quietly. Notice your thoughts and feelings. Breathe in and out. Clear your noisy head. You'll notice that you have thoughts, such as "The table needs dusting," "I forgot to put the field-trip permission slip in Josh's lunchbox" and "I need to send that e-mail." Don't focus on them. Picture the thoughts floating out of your head and drifting away. Don't pay any attention to them. Continue to breathe slowly. For just five short minutes, let the noise in your head quiet down. Later, talk together about the experience.

4. Practice. Most things in life need to be practiced; that's how our brains work. The noodle learns by experience. No experience and no practicing results in—you guessed it—no learning. So practice being in the moment. Go to a museum together. Focus on a painting or sculpture for a while and really look at it. No, we mean really looking at it. Drink the object in. Later, discuss what you each observed. Marti and her friend Val once looked at a Picasso together and at the

exact same moment they both burst out laughing. They had both seen a fried egg painted on the subject's forehead. It's a moment they get a kick out of remembering together.

Being present is that simple—it means just checking in with yourself moment to moment. Sustaining awareness across a stretch of time connects you with yourself and your life. Taking it moment by moment and becoming more alive isn't as hard as you might think.

Lend a Hand During Changes

Life transitions are experienced as quite stressful by most innies and some outies. Most innies like the familiar because they use less energy living a predictable life. And most life transitions require tanks of energy in order for introverts to handle them. This is because shifts require moving beyond the familiar, and they may also require more extroverting than the person is accustomed to doing. Changes burn fuel quickly because they are nerve wracking, they involve sudden shifts, and they require learning new things, making decisions, preparing, and practice (Brebner 1998). One of the more difficult changes for innies to handle is a shift in their circle of friends; and, since innies may make friends slowly and selectively it is difficult to lose friends during life changes. Sometimes innies shut down and withdraw when their lives change.

IMPACT OF CHANGES ON INNIES

Recently, Marti has really been reminded of how much energy big changes require. In 2005, we moved to Portland, Oregon, after living in Los Angeles for more than thirty years. Even though LA was crowded and hectic, at least she knew her way around. But Portland is completely unfamiliar to her, and she has trouble driving anywhere in our new city without getting lost. "I don't have any of my familiar stomping grounds," she says. "I've been laughing at myself and realizing that it's really true—the unfamiliar is very exhausting." Trisha, an innie friend who still lives in Los Angeles, says, "I am never moving. Nathan and I talk about dying in our house. I love the familiar."

Even small changes can affect innies, because they need to adjust to any change by retrieving former memories and experiences stored in their long-term memory. As a result, sometimes they are out of sync with the present. An innie client of Marti's went to Minnesota for three weeks when her mother became ill. When she returned home she was surprised to find that she felt somewhat disoriented. Even though Los Angeles had been her home for twenty years, nothing seemed familiar and she felt a bit lost. The feeling was a bit disconcerting, but thankfully it lifted within a couple of weeks.

It's important for outies to realize that changes overwhelm their innie partners, and that innies can really use their partners' help during changes. Outies can help by maintaining stability and leading the way during transitions, and by asking what their partners need from them.

Outies can remind innies to do the following things:

- Take time to breathe, rest, and remember that they will adjust.

- Take breaks.

- Think of past adjustments they have made.

- Talk with an old friend and make a new one.

- Break projects into baby steps.

- Keep familiar things, pictures, or mementoes that they love in sight.

- See if they can find something to enjoy about the change.

IMPACT OF CHANGES ON OUTIES

In general, outies get a kick out of changes. In fact, they may stir them up if no changes pop up naturally. New people coming into their lives may be easy for outies to handle because they make friends easily and see lots of folks as potential pals. Changes generate gobs of fuel for outies. But if a change is a result of a loss, they can respond by sidestepping the grieving process. Instead, they may get involved in a flurry of activity. Of course, if they ignore their losses they will miss out on deepening their capacity to feel painful emotions, and they won't learn and mature as a result of their life experiences.

Too many changes can become overwhelming even for outies. They may flame out from burning too much midnight oil. Changes that are affronts to their view of themselves (like getting fired or demoted) can decrease their confidence. Lower self-esteem increases a sense of being out of control, triggering fear and anger. Sometimes they blame others for changes they don't like.

Innie partners can encourage their outies to slow down and cool their jets. If you're an innie, let your extrovert partner know that everything doesn't need to get done at once, and that changes take time. Don't catch your partner's anxiety, but acknowledge his or her feelings of anger, uncertainty, or fear.

Innies, remind outies to do the following:

- Slow down and pause to check in with themselves.

- Decide on priorities.

- Limit the change; don't add to it.

- Grieve, because we all suffer losses; sadness is normal and healthy.

- Stay the course; don't get ahead of themselves.

- Encourage and appreciate their efforts.

Flow-and-Grow Cycle

Throughout life we all keep working through basic questions: Who am I? Where am I going? What's important to me? What have I learned? What is the meaning of my life? What is my purpose? Each chapter of your life is defined by a shift of priorities, values, and purpose. The similar yet different chapters fold together into your life story. If you stay curious, you may see your life as a kaleidoscope turning—with colored chips falling into surprising and constantly shifting designs. When transitions occur, we respond, make choices, and move on. The result may be that you choose a new design for your life. It's unfamiliar at first, but you gradually become accustomed to the new patterns. In fact, you may find your energy in the fresh color combinations in the new design. So how do we learn to flow and grow through life transitions? We regenerate by processing the phases of change. Let's follow Nick and Debbie as they hop on the "flow-and-grow cycle."

PHASE 1: DREAMS OF THE FUTURE

In this stage, people have a dream or vision of their future. They may have a plan about how to achieve their dreams and goals. They launch themselves into their plans in order to meet their goals. After a while, they may plateau at this phase.

Nick, an extrovert, went to college and majored in marketing. He hit the ground running when he graduated, quickly achieving his dream of becoming the youngest marketing manager in his company. He enjoyed the fast pace of his job and was eager to continue climbing the promotional ladder. Although he was happy in his marriage, he focused on his career. His wife, Debbie, an introvert, felt that she had already achieved her dreams. She worked part-time as a children's librarian, she loved her husband, and she got a kick out of her two children. Although she was busy, her work and family activities fit her temperament and desires perfectly. She expected Nick to slow his pace soon.

PHASE 2: DOWN IN THE DOLDRUMS

People enter this phase when they feel they are in decline, they feel trapped, and negative emotions are erupting. They may feel angry, disappointed, discouraged, or frustrated. This may send them back to phase 1, where they dream up a plan for the future. If so, the life change will be only a slight shift, like minor surgery, because they haven't stopped to pay attention to their deeper feelings or reflect on their life or their gifts. This is a cycle many extroverts travel, never growing or developing fully. This phase can also be activated by a positive event, such as a promotion at work. Despite its exciting aspects, a positive change is still a change, so it can trigger feelings of loss, produce conflicts, and result in depression.

When Nick got a promotion, he was excited and proud of his achievement. Debbie wasn't quite so thrilled, and Nick didn't understand her reaction. He was going to be making more money, traveling more, and getting exposure to company higher-ups. He was walking on air. At the same time, energy was draining out of Debbie's toes when she thought of Nick being away more. She already felt she was stretched thin with her job, the house, and the children. Her dreams of Nick having more family time felt like they were fading away. She felt guilty and angry. Nick wanted Debbie to be proud and happy about his promotion, and he started feeling annoyed at her.

PHASE 3: COCOONING AND INTROSPECTION

This is a phase of turning inward to take stock of your life, an opportunity to assess your basic values and beliefs. In this phase you may feel stuck, unmotivated, tired, and depressed. And this may actually be a good thing, since depression helps us slow down so we can recover and start anew. Contrary to how our culture views losses, experts suggest that it takes up to two years to recover from a job loss, divorce, or any other major change. It's like major surgery. It can result in personal growth, new choices, and transformations, but you have to give yourself a lot of resting time in order to begin a new phase. Practicing this phase gives people great resiliency. Introverts, who can get stuck in this phase, are often reluctant to take the next risky step.

Even though Debbie had hired a sitter to help her out since Nick was traveling so much, she fell into a depression after his promotion. But since Nick was gone a lot he didn't notice. Debbie realized she had to take action, because she was miserable.

PHASE 4: RESTARTING & PRACTICING

At a certain point in phase 3 you will feel able to restart your life and move on. But don't rush and force a new beginning—you need to experience some disruption and confusion before you can see where you want your life to go. Being in limbo isn't pleasant, but it's a valuable place from which to examine your life. Readjust your priorities and develop new goals before heading in a new direction. If outies reach this phase, they may dash through it or act impulsively, doing things like buying a new car, going on an expensive trip, or remodeling their house, in order to force themselves to feel better about their decisions. Innies typically linger before deciding to act. Sometimes they need to motivate themselves to get going even when they know where they want to go.

Debbie finally told Nick they needed to have a talk. She told him she needed some changes. She was enjoying her alone time and the help she had hired but she wanted Nick to travel less. She also wanted him to help out on the weekends. Telling Nick what she wanted was a growth step for Debbie. Nick felt pressured by her requests, but discussing alternatives with Debbie threw some light on his own goals. He realized he was missing too much at home and that he did want to slow down a bit. Nick and Debbie felt stronger as a team as they worked out these problems.

PHASE 5: GOALS

Aim for attainable goals you really want. Are you both willing to spend the energy, time, and resources to reach your goals? When you reach your goals will you have gained more than you've lost? Do your goals fit with your basic values? Here are some steps to assist goal setting:

- Write down your goals—remember that you aren't carving them in stone.

- Break goals into steps—small targets are energizing.

- Review the steps you've decided on that will allow you to obtain your goals, and think about what works and what doesn't.

- Start now, even if you don't feel quite ready, and adjust as needed.

- Motivation usually comes after we take a few steps.

- Give yourselves incentives or rewards along the way, not just one at the end.

Debbie and Nick both grew as a result of taking a spin around the flow-and-grow cycle. Debbie initiated her own personal goals instead of leaving major life decisions up to Nick. And Nick broadened himself when he adjusted his personal goals to take his family's needs into account. Nick and Debbie now know they can handle future life transitions.

Tipping Points

Sometimes only one person in a couple decides to change. Perhaps it's a personal growth choice a partner makes to shift the direction of his or her life. Maybe one person begins psychotherapy. These tipping points disrupt a couple's emotional balance. Usually couples don't even know they have an emotional balance; it's out of their awareness. But changes tend to upset the marital applecart.

—Kari & Brad—

Kari, an innie, lost more than one hundred pounds. She was so thrilled. Her outie husband, Brad, had originally encouraged her to lose weight. Now something surprising was happening. Kari was going out more with her gal pals and Brad was becoming angry, jealous, and possessive. The relationship was tipped out of balance. Brad's insecurity had been forced out into the open because Kari had changed. As Kari's insecurity decreased and she felt better about herself, Brad's underlying insecurity bubbled to the surface.

Innies and outies often create a well-balanced couple. The most common tipping point is the innie's desire for more airtime, decision-making input, or world experiences. Extroverts may appear secure and independent until their partner's growth rocks their emotional boat. If an outie can't take the innie's desire to change as a cue to do some of his or her own growing, the relationship may decline. The innie may decide to go it alone, or, occasionally, the extrovert may decide he or she wants a more outgoing partner. These breakups can be healthy for each of the individuals. But couples always have another choice. Tipping points can be opportunities to grow both personally and as a couple.

Lend a Helping Hand Every Day

Every day, innies and outies live through small changes. Moods, energy, and events change from moment to moment. Mornings and evenings are often periods when innies and outies are functioning at different tempos. In between, they each face tiny disappointments, frustrations, surprises, and changes that call for adaptations. Changes affect each partner differently. In response to changes, partners may find themselves wanting to change or fix some aspect of their spouse. However, the more couples accept themselves as a package deal with built-in gifts, problems, and transition styles, the more they can face what can and can't be changed.

Innies usually need to pace themselves more than outies do. Building in structure and predictability reduces the energy innies have to burn during change. Many innies and outies enter a new day at their own individual velocity. Introverts usually ease out of a fog and into their day at a slow pace. They may stagger toward their coffee and down it in one gulp in order to get a caffeine jolt. Light from lamps or windows helps to start their engines. Most innies aren't too chatty until they are fully awake. And because they start off slow, it's often better for innies to get everything ready the night before so their morning takeoff goes smoothly. It's important for them to have a good breakfast since they have metabolized food all night. Introverts need to fuel up for the day.

In the evening, innies may need to have some quiet time before sharing their day. Carving out fifteen minutes of quiet can make a big difference to an innie's evening; commuting can provide a bit of restorative solitude for an innie. Outies may get home full of vim and vigor. Some adapt easily to the hubbub at home; others need to take a few minutes to shift their emotional focus. However, occasionally the tables are turned and it's the outie who wants some peace and quiet after all that extroverting. And an innie spouse who was home all day with children might be disappointed because he or she was looking forward to an adult conversation.

—Alex & Laurie—

Extroverted Alex, married to introverted Laurie, says, "I have finally gotten used to Laurie's slow start in the morning. I have stopped pressuring her to chat." Outies often spring out of bed ready to face their day. They may want to discuss plans and decisions. They tend to hit the shower, get dressed, throw back some OJ, and bound out of the house, eager to hit the road. Laurie comments, "Alex drove me nuts when we were first married. He was so noisy in the morning. It was so irritating. I got him a shower radio so he can have a sing-along with others in the morning."

Remember, innies and outies react differently to the same daily events. See if you notice subtle changes in your moods, energy, and reactions throughout the day. Help your partner cope with small shifts. Noticing and adjusting to tiny changes can help release tension during the day. Use humor, thoughtfulness, and playfulness. And don't worry about the things that are really unimportant. Your relationship will be changed for the better.

Smooth Out Speed Bumps

Everyone who is alive experiences pressures, pains, and life changes. We all need to be able to smooth out our emotional reactions. In order to do this, we need to build and maintain relationships with people who are open about their thoughts and feelings. Caring partners are good listeners, give emotional support, and, if needed, can help you calm down. Partners can help each other regulate their emotional peaks and valleys. Some couples get into a pattern of coming home and spouting energy-draining complaints. We suggest creating a buffer zone, and trying a new way of greeting each other: Each of you will listen to a complaint about the day that is no more than twenty-five words long, such as "Man, what a frustrating day. I am so bushed." Then offer twenty-five or fewer positive words about the evening ahead, to balance your negative feelings with positive ones. "I am so glad to finally be home. It's great to see you all. Let's go for ice cream after dinner tonight."

Coping with Change

Below are some recommendations for how to deal with change in a positive way.

EXPECT CHANGE AND TRANSITIONS. Adjustments are needed every day in every way.

LEARN TO GRIEVE LOSSES. Each person copes with losses in his or her own way. Losses take time to grieve. Accepting the process of grieving is vital to managing life's ebbs and flows. Grieving processes our thoughts and feelings. Emotions are internal threads that knit our brain pathways together, which means that people who grieve losses develop more complex coping skills. Shock is the first stage of experiencing a loss. Next come feelings of denial, disbelief, numbness, hysteria, and incredulity. Protest then comes online, often followed by anger, guilt, sadness, fear, longing, and emptiness. Disorganization follows, and, with it comes a bleak feeling of despair, fatigue, confusion, apathy, and desolation. Last, reorganization begins when life starts to return to normal, but the person now resumes life with the awareness that the loss has changed him or her and brought maturity to his or her life.

FOCUS ON WHAT YOU ARE GRATEFUL FOR (EVEN THE SMALLEST THINGS). Each day brings so many gifts, if you notice them. A fresh, warm spring breeze, children's chalk drawings on the sidewalk, a friendly dog, a baby waving, people laughing, fresh laundry, cold water on a hot day, and cushy pillows.

SAY GOOD-BYE TO THE ILLUSION OF CONTROL— LIFE HOLDS SURPRISES. Change threatens our illusion of control. As helpless children we need this illusion. When we grow up we need to let that notion go because we don't really have control of life. Take heart, though, because we do have some amount of control over ourselves. Life runs its own course and people do their own things. But we do have choices about how we cope with what life sends our way. Paradoxically, we have more choices when we leave the illusion of control behind.

Four Quick Keys

We all need to make daily changes. You can change individually, help each other make a personal change, or make changes together. Here are the four quick keys to effective change:

First, and most important, decide to change. ("I will walk four times a week.")

Second, plan for trouble spots. ("If I don't feel like walking I'll call my friend for encouragement. I'll walk the next day without attacking myself. I will remember my goal.")

Third, sustain the new behavior. ("If I walk four times a week for a month, I can buy a new book and a new DVD.")

Fourth, congratulate yourself on your change. Tell others about your accomplishment, write "Good for you" in lipstick on your bathroom mirror, enjoy your walk, and notice how you feel—stronger and more in control of your own life. ♡

9

sticky wickets
when worlds collide

"Winning and losing are goals for games, not for conflicts.
Learning, growing, and cooperating are goals for resolving conflicts."
—Thomas Crum

Jung indicated that he thought conflicts were built in to the opposing forces of introverted and extroverted relationships. Conflicts have a bad name because they can be unsettling, scary, and destructive. Despite its negative associations, fighting can actually help relationships grow. Conflicts usually arise when fundamental values are threatened, like trust, independence, closeness, differences, values, power, control, and expressing love. Couples develop intimacy by working through conflicts, understanding each other better, and finding solutions to their difficulties.

Conflicts Affect the Whole Brain

Each section of the brain (front, back, left, and right) influences how we deal with conflicts. As you may recall from chapter 2, innies spend more time in the front of the brain and outies spend more time in the back of the brain. Both innies and outies will also use either their right (feeling) brain or their left (thinking) brain during arguments. When whole-brain differences are considered it's easy to see why misunderstandings escalate into conflicts. Accusations will begin to fly if you don't stop and consider your opposing viewpoints.

First, let's look at the different ways innies and outies deal with conflict. These opposing temperament differences make conflicts challenging because temperament influences many areas like body language, pacing, intensity, and internal processing. In general, innies want to discuss the conflict later and outies want to get right to it. When conflicts escalate, outies tend to move their bodies more and talk louder and faster. This is why driving the car or taking a walk while we're talking seems to help Mike release body tension. Walking or riding in the car also helps Marti feel like Mike is paying more attention to what she's saying. Introverts, on the other hand, grow still, pause between words, and speak in a quieter voice as conflicts escalate. They may become silent until they are clearer about their thoughts or feelings. It usually takes a lot of anger, frustration, and energy for innies to get to the point of yelling. Often innies reduce eye contact when they are upset because they are overwhelmed. Innies withdraw if they feel their partner isn't listening to them or tries to intimidate them.

Second, let's see how each hemisphere contributes to how conflicts are handled. Left-brained folks look at conflicts logically and right-brained people take the emotional approach. A left-brained person, usually male, tends to be uncomfortable with emotions and often becomes defensive. His body posture is closed: his arms are crossed, he doesn't appear to be listening, and he looks irritated. He is thinking about solutions while his spouse is talking, and he wants his ideas valued. A right-brained person, usually female, wants to connect emotionally before beginning to solve the issue. She wants her partner to understand how she feels. Emotions may escalate if her partner doesn't acknowledge her feelings. It does require effort and understanding to overcome these opposing approaches. It isn't easy. But that's exactly why the Venus and Mars books, which are based primarily on emotional versus logical brain differences, were so popular—these conflicts are very challenging.

LEFT-BRAINED PARTNERS

Left-brained folks focus on the practical aspects of conflict. It is helpful to be direct and succinct when talking with them, because they are linear and logical in their thinking. Emotions seem threatening and unnecessary to many left-brained folks—"Just the facts, ma'am." Listed below are left-brained viewpoints—what a left-brained partner pays attention to during a conflict:

- What the conflict is about
- Logic, opinions, and principles
- Succinct delivery
- Analyzing differences in a negative light
- Maintaining a firm stance
- Being right or wrong

The following are suggested ways to approach conflicts with your left-brained partner for a better result:

"I want to tell you about a problem and I would just like you to listen."

"I would like to talk about it for a few minutes."

"I'd like you to imagine how this has affected me."

"I'd like you to realize how I think and feel about this."

"What do you think about the situation?"

"What solutions do you see in the gray area between black and white?"

RIGHT-BRAINED PARTNERS

Right-brained partners are concerned about emotions and the people aspect of conflicts. Emotions must be acknowledged before they will embark on finding practical solutions. Listed below are their viewpoints —what they focus on during a conflict:

- Who is involved

- Partner's needs and values

- Accepting and appreciating differences

- Tactful delivery

- Ensuring give and take

- Respecting each other's viewpoints, feelings, and ideas

Use the questions and statements below when conflicts arise with right-brained folks—you'll get a much better outcome:

"What are you feeling?"

"What concerns you the most about this situation?"

"You're saying that you feel _____." (Acknowledge their emotions—you need not have the same feelings.)

"Are you feeling better? What are your thoughts? Are you ready to problem-solve?"

"These are just choices. Whether we are right or wrong, we can always make other decisions later."

WHAT GENERATES CONFLICTS

Conflict inevitably arises in any relationship between two people, each with different wants and needs. An innie's tendency to withdraw and an outie's propensity to overpower easily create frustrations. And right- or left-brain orientations throw extra spice into the conflict pot. Let's take a look at the conflict generators for all four profiles, and examine some ways to learn from your tussles.

Conflict Generators for Right-Brained Innies

- Disruption to their sense of connection and belonging
- Teasing, ridiculing, and critical vibes
- Being asked to deal with too many details or rigid expectations
- Partner's disregard for their emotional content or values
- Feeling overwhelmed by too much extroverting
- Having insufficient time to discuss important issues
- Feeling ignored, not listened to, or walked on
- Feeling hopeless or discouraged

"Marti senses unspoken tension in those around her," Mike observes. "Her emotions are not always apparent to me. She likes to hear all sides of a conflict before reaching a decision. She knows her own perceptions but she is open to others' views. She doesn't usually engage in conflict unless she feels strongly about something. A conflict trigger for her is a challenge to her values or an impact on her important relationships. She wants everyone to be heard and included. She listens respectfully but doesn't jump to conclusions. She feels some things are worth fighting for, and others are not. She notices and accepts feelings, both hers and others'. To her, a good outcome to a conflict is one that involves an open exploration, with both people airing opinions and views, and one that doesn't necessarily bring the conflict to resolution or closure. She avoids fighting and withdraws if the quarrel is prolonged. After a fight she wants us to repair the relationship and learn from the conflict."

Conflict Generators for Left-Brained Innies

- Feeling pressure to wing it; not having enough time to reflect
- Partner's lack of follow-through on agreed-upon decisions or changes
- Being asked to justify their actions or choices; having others challenging their authority
- Emotional turbulence in relationship
- Intrusions into personal space; partner talking too much
- Not having enough time to discuss important matters; outie partner setting the pace
- Common sense being ignored by outie partner

"During a fight Carlos is hard to read, because he doesn't show his feelings," states his wife, Teresa. "Often he is very frustrating because he plays the devil's advocate. He takes the side of any underdog and questions all assumptions. I'm struggling to piece my words together. I end up feeling like I'm in court defending myself. He doesn't seem engaged in the problem *with* me. He wants to win the fight and ignores my feelings. He wants me to trust him and believe him but he doesn't always trust me. He wants to get the fight over with quickly because he sees problems as a waste of time. But when the conflict is over he won't let it go. It drives me crazy. He usually thinks he's right. And you know where that leaves me. Occasionally he will admit that his attitude contributed to the fight. His logic is helpful at times but usually he's concerned with defending himself, not working together as a team."

Conflict Generators for Left-Brained Outies

- Making assumptions without checking with their partner
- Feeling questioned about their abilities or behaviors
- Feeling slighted, criticized, or judged unfairly
- Others challenging their authority, opinions, or ideas
- Partner's or others' emotions; illogical arguments
- Feeling emotionally cut off from their partner
- Innie partner's reluctance to decide or take action
- Feeling out of control, vulnerable, or powerless

Marti says, "Mike does show his emotional reactions, although often subtly. He approaches conflicts with a coolheaded, analytical approach and has difficulty staying with the emotional side of conflicts. He wants me to see the beauty of his left-brained, logical thinking. Questioning his authority triggers anger. He resists conflicts and thinks we shouldn't have them. If we do have a fight, he wants it to be over ASAP. My emotions trigger his and he feels flooded. He shifts from easygoing to angry quickly if he begins to feel overwhelming emotions. He feels out of control and helpless. Mike can be aggressive when he wants problems solved. His main goal is to make a decision and end the conflict."

Conflict Generators for Right-Brained Outies

- Being prevented from doing something, especially something that's fun

- Feeling railroaded, fenced in, or restricted
- Feeling that their values are being disrespected by others
- Overreaction from a partner who is questioning their loyalty
- Unwillingness by their innie partner to resolve differences
- Experiencing harshness or intentional harm from someone they trust

Jim, one of the innie partners we interviewed, says, "Others notice Sue's emotional reactions. She is expressive, warm, and caring but she hates tension and she always wants harmony. If her core beliefs are challenged she may fight. She is always concerned about how conflicts affect her relationships. She can be emotional and intense but she doesn't want her relationships damaged. She wants us to clear the air so we don't harbor resentments. She feels we can resolve anything if we are honest and open about our feelings. She doesn't understand why I can't talk conflicts over immediately. Her goal is open communication. She delays our decisions if others are concerned, and it's frustrating for me at times."

Creating a Cooperative Connection

As you have seen, it is very easy to generate conflicts. To maintain a strong connection, couples can learn to move from conflict into cooperation. Cooperation means working together to bridge your natural gaps and find mutually satisfying solutions. Couples don't keep their dukes up quite as long when they view annoying behaviors as natural differences to be understood. Defensiveness is lowered when partners are interested in listening to each other's viewpoints and are willing to give up some of their own needs or wishes. Resolutions to disagreements are easily found when both partners' thoughts and feelings are taken into account.

This attitude of goodwill and cooperation is an invaluable foundation for repairing and resolving problems as they arise.

When you are both feeling relaxed and open is a good time to discuss your reactions to conflicts. What are your normal patterns? Most introverts tend to withdraw, because conflicts trigger adrenaline and dopamine, which they find overstimulating. However, they usually come back later to discuss the issues because they don't like unresolved conflicts—they are uncomfortable with the residual tension crackling in the air. On the other hand, many outies love a good, exciting fight. And they may even start them without realizing it, since quarrels pump dopamine, adrenaline, and other chemical shots of intensity into their bodies. Sometimes extroverts may prefer to avoid emotional and complex problems requiring longer discussions. Discuss what your patterns are. Talk about how to handle conflicts with an attitude of cooperation.

One of the biggest barriers to cooperation is its opposite: competition. When you and your spouse are competitive, the goal is to defend yourself and attack your partner ("I must win"). Many extroverts tend to compete and resist compromise. Competing places a high priority on one's own interests. Compromising means each party sacrifices some of their wants and needs, and cooperating includes each person's needs and wants. What do you tend to do? Do you fight to win? Do you try to understand and cooperate? Seeing your partner as an ally instead of a competitor will make conflict resolution easier and enhance your relationship.

Here's another way to think about competition: it's actually an attempt to handle conflicts without experiencing emotions. It's a thinking strategy. So, instead of taking the thinking approach, notice your feelings. You'll find that problems are solved quickly when your underlying emotions are addressed. The best decisions and plans are made when thoughts and feelings are integrated. Ratchet down your defenses and don't take conflicts so personally. You might even learn something.

CONFLICT-CLOBBERING TECHNIQUES

We all have disputes. What makes a relationship healthy is how you settle disagreements. Below, we propose some techniques that both innies and outies can use to resolve conflicts. We have found these techniques useful over many years of marriage, but keep in mind that these are just examples. Use your own words if the ones we suggest don't seem right. Remember, it can be tough to remain open if emotions are running high. But keep at it, because *repairing* your relationship is the most important thing when you're involved in a conflict with your partner. Practice these seven steps to resolving conflicts. Trust us, it gets easier.

1. If you are an outie, say,

   "May I have your attention now to talk about this problem? If not, when will you feel ready to talk about it?"

   If you are an innie, say,

   "Are you available to talk about this problem?"

   If you are left brained, say,

   "This is something important to me. I'd like to talk about it logically first without discussing solutions, although I have thought of some."

   If you are right brained, say,

   "I want to take a moment to consider this and how it affects us before I respond. I do want to hear your logical explanations. Please also listen to my emotional concerns."

2. Clarify the conflict—make sure you establish what you are fighting about.

3. Find out what you both agree on.

4. Listen carefully to each other and stay calm during the discussion.

5. Speak from your own viewpoint—explain your thoughts and feelings—and take turns.

6. Restate your partner's viewpoint—did you understand your partner's thoughts and feelings? Ask for feedback.

7. Adopt a curious and cooperative attitude—in effect, sidestep feeling personally attacked. Attack the problem, not each other.

CONFLICT STICKERS

After Mike and I had been married a few years we began to notice a pattern with our fights. We would get stuck and replay the same conflicts over and over. We assigned numbers to each fight. We were then able to shorten our battles by laughing and saying, "Oh, this is fight number sixty-three—we know how it turns out." Listed below are some of the "sticky wickets" that contribute to recurring fights. We also offer tips to unstick the conflicts.

Body Talk

Remember the discussion in chapter 4 about nonverbal communication? It is critical to notice your own body posture during conflicts. Congruent verbal and nonverbal communication is vital. When the two don't match, your partner won't experience you as trustworthy, authentic, or involved. Also notice your partner's tone of voice, body language, and feelings. Fights can reoccur when verbal and nonverbal communication don't match, because these reflect underlying issues that aren't being addressed. Aim to be congruent in both forms of communication.

CONGRUENT BODY TALK

- Stand upright but not rigid, leaning forward with upper body open.

- Maintain eye contact; show you are listening.

- Breathe slowly, taking in the information presented.

- Relax—tension can build up during conflicts.

- Have a relaxed stance; this shows openness to hearing another's point of view.

- Restate what you hear. Express your opinions. Long-winded lecturing (typical of outies) is off-putting.

- Lower the pitch of your voice; this automatically forces you to slow down. However, don't slow down so much that you sound condescending.

MISMATCHED BODY TALK

- Crossed arms imply that you are defensive and closed. Open up your arms.

- Defensive postures make you look disinterested or hostile. Remember, this is your loving partner and the goal is to resolve issues. Show interest.

- Lack of eye contact tells innies that you are not listening. No eye contact is usually accepted by outies, as long as you show some signs that you are listening and caring.

Mind Reading

Check your crystal ball at the door. Assuming what your partner means without checking it out with him or her causes the majority of recurring fights. It's easy to believe we know what others think or feel. And our brain-hemisphere dominance and temperament can contribute to this tendency toward mind reading. Outies often think they know others' intentions, while innies sometimes question their own motivations. Left-brained partners tend to think they know what their spouses think, and right-brained partners pick up feelings that the other person may not be aware of. Check out your assumptions about your partner's thoughts and feelings. Listen to his or her perceptions about him- or herself and feedback about you—especially if your partner is better at noticing emotions. Stay curious. Remember that the majority of our brain activity is unconscious, so we all need help to understand what and how we are communicating.

Dismissing

Not paying attention to your partner's reactions prevents you from developing empathy for your partner as he or she struggles with the problem at hand. Rolling your eyes, hurling insults, staying defensive, and making dismissive comments are all hurtful and only create more conflict.

EMOTIONAL FLOODING

Due to their dopamine-based physiology, extroverts become more animated during fights. Their voices get louder and their bodies more active. They can become more physically aggressive in order to make their points. Quite often, they are unable to receive input, despite the good intentions they may have. Introverts, on the other hand, tend to protect their feelings and retreat. If they don't feel listened to they may not express their opinions. Consequently, outies may become self-righteous and dig in their heels, and innies may shut down without taking the risk to speak. This is not a good combo. Remember the dance metaphor we discussed in chapter 3? In the case of unresolved conflict, partners are dancing out of step to their own music. Here are some suggestions to help you learn to dance to the same tune:

Don't discuss an upsetting topic when you're tired, flooded with emotion, or stressed about something else.

Suggest going on a walk in a scenic area, or just around the block, and use this time to talk. Be tactful and make an effort to acknowledge your partner's efforts. Reduce escalation by blending thoughts and feelings.

If the fight begins to escalate, take a thirty-minute break. Be respectful, not degrading, of your partner if he or she needs this time. Taking the time to calm down will lead to better talks and better conflict resolution. If tempers get too hot you can always postpone the discussion to the following day. To avoid emotional flooding, all discussions should have agreed-upon time limits.

Depending upon the depth and importance of the issue, it may take a while for you to resolve it. Meet again, and again, and again if necessary in order to resolve the discussion.

Work together to maintain a dialogue—let your partner know what's going on with you. Focus on the positives in your relationship.

LEADERS & FOLLOWERS

Studies show that extroverts are often the captain of the ship and introverts are the first mates (Caprara 1994). Most relationships have areas where one person leads and the other follows. This works fine if you each have your own spheres of power, you are both flexible, and the power division isn't too extreme. It becomes destructive when people in power always want their way, must be right, and avoid working cooperatively with their partners. If one person is in control indefinitely, the less-dominant spouse will eventually become depressed, engage in passive-aggressive behavior, or give up. This issue is on the rise today and can lead to abuse and violence, so it's important for you to discuss power and control in your relationship. It can be an insidious problem, slowly increasing until one partner is demoralized. If you work together, and decide issues respectfully together, then the balance of power and control won't be a problem.

Grow Toward Mutual Relating

Listed below are some questions to reflect on and talk over together. If you have control issues, these questions can help you gain perspective. Becoming conscious of how each partner's power and control issues affect the other will help both of you. We hope you have a good discussion.

- List the positive and negative traits of your parents. List your positive and negative traits. Now list your partner's positive and negative traits. Do you notice any patterns? How did your parents deal with conflicts, control, and power? What did you learn from them?

- List the traits you like least in your partner. What traits do you like best in your partner? Can your partner listen to your feedback?

- How do you handle frustrations? Do you nag? Withdraw? Ignore your partner? Attack? Boss? Feel that you are right? In general, do you play up conflicts or play down conflicts?

- Ask your partner what bugs him or her most about you. Ask what he or she would like from you. Listen without countering, interrupting, or defending yourself. Step into your partner's shoes. Validate his or her point of view, but remember that you need not agree.

- Keep in mind that you are acting in a controlling way if you cut your partner off or dismiss his or her opinions, feelings, or viewpoint.

- An important word of caution: Don't be open and vulnerable with your partner if he or she isn't honest, caring, and vulnerable with you. ♡

10

harnessing your strengths
team up when stepping out

"What do we live for if it is not to make life less
difficult for each other?" —George Eliot

Mike and Marti settle into the car. Mike starts the engine and
a gust of oldies music blasts from the car radio. Marti's ears reverberate;
she jumps and yelps. This isn't a new scene—it has happened before:
Mike forgot to turn down the radio, and the loud music hurts Marti's
ears. This kind of difference is just the tip of the iceberg between introverts and extroverts when they step out into the world. Just about everything introverts and extroverts do when they are out and about exposes
their contrasting temperaments.

We hope that by this point in the book you know and accept yourself
and your partner with more appreciation. Understanding and accepting
yourself is the ticket to increased self-confidence. Moving out into the
world is easier when you feel confident, know that you can rely upon

yourself, and know that you have support from your partner. And partners who know each other well can harness their advantages to support each other out in the world.

The term "extrovert" comes from Latin, meaning "outward turning." Outies want to jump into activity. They are admired and valued by others so their self-confidence is buoyed. "Introvert," also from Latin, means "inward turning." Introverts want to have a clear idea of what's happening before they leap out into the fray. When introverts go extroverting they need to turn themselves inside out. Leaving their inner world and facing a completely different outside world can be overstimulating for them. Everything they do in the outside world takes gallons of energy. Innies usually feel misunderstood and underappreciated, so being out in the world often lowers their self-confidence (Golden 1994). Your outward or inward orientation influences your occupation, parenting, exercise or sport preferences, and feeling of connectedness when you step out into the world.

Nine to Five

Because you probably spend a great deal of your waking time at work, it's important to have a job that is satisfying and nourishes most aspects of your temperament. Many occupations allow both innies and outies to perform work in their own way. For instance, teaching works for both temperaments, although they will each have their own approach. For example, when Marti teaches she prefers small classes. She tends to first lecture based on lengthy reading assignments; she discourages interruptions but encourages discussions of different points of view later on in the course. When Mike teaches he gives brief reading assignments and encourages immediate discussions, group projects, and lots of questions and interruptions.

JOBS FOR INNIES

Innies try to understand the world before they experience it, so they are pulled toward mental activity. Introverts tend to enjoy jobs where they can use their ability to concentrate, explore a subject in depth, work alone, and use their one-on-one relational skills. They want a workplace where their ideas are valued and they can work in privacy without interruptions. Occupations that allow flexible schedules work best for innies, so they can recharge when needed. Words associated with innies include "assimilator," "visionary," "analyzer," and "enhancer." For example, Jennifer, an innie, enjoys staying in her office and using her expertise to thoroughly investigate and integrate information for her reports. She likes to have enough time to carefully research and prepare documents. Coworkers see her as reliable, knowledgeable, quiet, and calm. She is usually fairly reticent in meetings, but when she does speak she makes a lot of sense and her coworkers respect her opinion. Jobs that are attractive to introverts include the following: artist, assistant, preschool teacher, programmer, librarian, architect, auditor, college professor, accountant, engineer, writer, researcher, and certain types of sales positions.

Innies' Job Strengths

In calmer, slower-paced environments, innies will bring invaluable strengths to their workplace. Below are a few of those strengths:

- They plan and set goals well.
- They reflect before suggesting ideas.
- They write well, usually from in-depth knowledge.
- They delve into subjects in detail and want to learn.
- They are self-motivated and don't have to be persuaded if interested in the subject.
- They listen well and take in information from all sources.

Innies' Blind Spots

When the work setting is unsuited to innies, such as a fast-paced, team-oriented company, challenges like the following may arise for them:

- They may not act quickly on ideas.

- They may not show others their thought process or explain how they came up with solutions.

- They may isolate themselves and forget to get input from others.

- They may not immediately recognize when quicker, simpler answers are required.

JOBS FOR OUTIES

Outies need to experience the world in order to understand it, so they are pulled toward people and activities. Outies enjoy jobs that have lots of variety, meetings, group planning and problem solving, action, people contact, and out-of-the-office appointments. Words that describe outies in the workplace might be "responder," "explorer," "expeditor," and "contributor." For example, Jim, an outie, enjoys discussing problems, solutions, and decisions with his coworkers. He likes to talk until he gets clearer about solutions and ideas. He enjoys a fast-paced environment with lots going on and constant change. Coworkers see him as a team player, energetic, and competent. He likes to wing it when approaching situations he hasn't extensively prepared for. He feels comfortable with interruptions, phone calls, and meetings and usually speaks up in groups. Jobs that attract extroverts include the following: marketer, public relations specialist, teacher, attorney, human resources manager, nurse, salesperson, manager, and speaker.

Outies' Job Strengths

In the right environment, outies' strengths can shine, as listed below:

- They are natural team players and networkers.
- They are willing to take quick action and make decisions.
- They are strong team motivators. ·
- They can speak and think quickly on their feet.
- They can shift subjects easily.

Outies' Blind Spots

In work settings that are slower and require complex assessments before implementation of plans, outies may experience the following challenges:

- They may talk too much and may not pick up social cues that others are ready to end a discussion.
- They may act without enough information and make decisions too hastily.
- They may not listen to others' input.
- They may become defensive if criticized.
- They may easily change their mind after receiving new input and may not stick to their convictions.

SUPPORT YOUR LOCAL PARTNER

Encourage each other's career development. Don't let your partner forget his or her strengths, and gently remind him or her to work on those blind spots. Remind each other to keep your advantages and challenges in mind when preparing a resumé or looking at job requirements. Celebrate each other's successes. You are a team!

DAY-TO-DAY HELPING

All of us have good and bad days at work, even if we love our work. As we all know, today most jobs require longer hours and come with more pressure. Frustrations can drive a wedge into your relationship. Or they can bring you together. Discuss with your partner how you feel about your job. Do you feel that it's a good fit? What do you like? What don't you like? What works well for you at your job and what doesn't? Is your boss an innie or an outie? Are you keeping that in mind when you interact with your boss and your coworkers?

When it's time to plan a change in your career, you and your partner can buy some books on career change. Make a date to work on a step-by-step plan together. It can be fun. Ask for your partner's support with your job search. Explain your challenges at work. Ask your partner to brainstorm solutions. There are many ways you can champion, balance, and teach each other. The couples in the following paragraphs exemplify ways partners can use their gifts to encourage each other at work.

—Jim & Haley—

Jim, an outie, helps his wife, Haley, an innie trainer, to prepare before giving a new workshop. Jim acts as her audience while she practices her presentation. He asks questions and has fun playing the "big mouth" one finds in most classes. On her work calendar he jots "Take a break" in red pen and draws a heart around it. He gently reminds her to blow her own horn and e-mail her ideas to her boss after a meeting. Jim looks forward to Haley's company social events and encourages her to go. He also tosses into a discussion, "Have you discussed your project with Bob? He would probably be interested." When Jim comes home and Haley is lying facedown on the sofa, he diverts the kids, covers her with a quilt, and starts dinner.

Jim is a manager of a large sports store. His job is fast paced and demanding. Haley helps him prioritize his tasks, because everything seems urgent to him and he's always torn. He is good with customers but he easily gets ticked off when customers are dishonest or rude. Haley tames Jim's temper and reminds him to step back and depersonalize irritating customers. She also reminds him to take a lunch break, say no to his boss occasionally, and step outside for a breath of fresh air when he needs to. She knows Jim becomes overwhelmed at work. Once he arrives home she reminds him to forget about his job, slow down, and do nothing for at least thirty minutes.

—Diane & Beth—

Both Diane, an innie, and Beth, an outie, are saleswomen. In fact, they met at work. Beth discusses strategy for her territory with Diane because Diane is good at thinking ahead and remembering what happened in the past. Diane reminds Beth to listen instead of guessing about her customers' concerns. She suggests ways Beth might improve her working relationships. Diane reminds Beth to check in without pressuring her innie customers.

Beth encourages Diane to take credit for all the work she produces and gives her tips about asserting herself with aggressive people. On the weekends, Beth tackles errands so Diane can stay home and recharge. She answers phone calls and speaks to coworkers when Diane is too pooped to pop. Beth reminds Diane to show more expression, lean forward and make direct eye contact, speak faster and louder, and use shorter sentences when she's in a meeting surrounded by outies. She also encourages Diane to pass out compliments freely.

Parenting Partners

Raising and disciplining children quickly reveal clashes over values that are tough to handle. Innies and outies can come to blows over childrearing issues. However, partners in an innie-outie duo also complement each other's strengths. When innie and outie parents work well together they solve problems easily. They offer their children the best of both worlds. One secret to compatible parenting is to balance values. Working together shows children that it's okay to have different values, strengths, and challenges, that it's okay to be who they are. The family is stronger because everyone contributes their separate perspectives.

Discuss your children's temperaments and how you picture them as adults—do they seem more introverted or extroverted? Discuss with your spouse how you wish your child would turn out as an adult. This view of the future gives you a peek into your own values. Place your imaginary pictures side by side and notice how similar or different they are. Do you want your child to be honest? Have a hobby? Be loving and giving? Religious? Self-confident? A jock? Popular? Would you like your child to help others? Become educated? Enter a profession? Make lots of money? Get married? Have children? Do you hope your child travels? Plays a musical instrument? Is an innie or an outie?

HERE COMES THE JUDGE

Raising children stirs strong emotions in parents. It sets off a roller coaster of anger, love, frustration, delight, confusion, and enjoyment. And this can be difficult to deal with, because our culture frowns on emotions. For this reason, it's important to appreciate yourself, whether you're a thinking or a feeling parent. Keep in mind that no one is an expert parent. Parenting requires a delicate balance between focusing on our own thoughts and feelings and those of our children.

Each child is a seed with an innate potential to grow, flourish, and bloom in his or her own unique way. No parent can make a tulip into an iris. Trouble starts when parents judge temperaments and try to make children act like something they're not. Your children's self-confidence is undermined when they feel it's wrong to be an innie or outie. Parents, like good gardeners, can only provide the environment where each seed germinates, unfolds, develops, and finally blossoms into the flower it is destined to be.

Although parents need to be in charge, see if you can reduce your inclination to control, manage, or direct your children when possible. Balance your responses by occasionally letting them get their way when appropriate, compromising at other times, and saying no when needed. Respect your children's thoughts and feelings and listen to their opinions.

Similarly, how parents treat each other is critical to how your children feel about themselves and others. Everyone is unique, and parents come in many styles. Moms and dads, as introverts and extroverts, offer different strengths to children. You'll feel most successful at parenting when you accept the different styles, temperaments, and strengths of your parenting partner and your children.

It is helpful for you and your spouse to discuss the principles that you think are the most important in parenting. Discuss temperaments and how they affect family members. Try to stay curious and nonjudgmental—this kind of conversation is meant to help you feel better about parenting. In the end, you'll know that you can turn to your partner for support in areas where you have trouble.

PRODUCTIVE PARENTING DISCUSSIONS

Here are five questions that may help each of you initiate a parenting discussion:

1. How is your child unique?

2. How is your child's temperament different from or similar to your own?

3. Is it easy or hard to listen to and speak your child's language?

4. Are you aware of how cultural biases influence your view of your child?

5. Do you assign negative motivations, rather than temperament influences, to your child's behavior?

—Sara & James—

Sara and James imagined that their children would be little carbon copies of themselves. James was an accountant who tended to be an easygoing, strong, silent type. His wife, Sara, was outgoing, energetic, and talkative. Their first baby, Abby, was quiet, pensive, and emotionally intense. She was independent, observant, and stubborn. Their next child, Ellie, was the life of the party. She was eager to please and excitable. She didn't like to play alone, chatted all day, and loved the limelight. Sara and James were thrown for a loop. They didn't know how to parent children who were so different.

Sara was comfortable encouraging Ellie's love of activity and interaction. James loved Ellie but he found her draining at times. James found it easier to give space to Abby so she could play or read alone. He wasn't annoyed when Abby didn't say hello to him when she came home from school. But Sara felt hurt. She found Abby's slower pace tiring and frustrating at times. Sara and James decided to use what they had learned about their own temperaments and apply it to parenting their two very different daughters. They decided to encourage Abby to at least wave to her mom when she got home, since James explained that Abby was feeling exhausted from a long day at school. For her part, Sara explained to James how hard it was for Ellie to be quiet, and that she really needed praise and attention. James got better at complimenting Ellie. He also practiced asking her to listen to the radio in the car without talking for ten or fifteen minutes. As a result of their teamwork, Sara and James felt more effective as parents and more supported by each other.

INNIE & OUTIE PARENTING GIFTS

How can parents like Sara and James and others learn to pool their resources and parent children with different temperaments? You can be effective if you parent as a team. By knowing your own temperament and that of your coparent, you now can blend your strengths, avoid blind spots, and appreciate your children for who they are. In the pages that follow, we will first discuss your parenting strengths and then we'll look at how you can support each other.

Innie parents:

- Are observant and know their child in depth
- Protect their child's private time
- Appreciate individuality
- Create a calm and quiet environment
- Focus on the family and tune out distractions
- Give the child space for outside relationships

Outie parents:

- Know and show the world to the child
- Motivate and encourage
- Invite people into the family
- Are involved in activities
- Are social and teach interpersonal skills
- Enjoy chitchat

If your spouse is an outie, you might remind him or her to:

- Join a group or find other ways to stay connected with other adults

- Practice saying no
- Stay home alone once a week to balance outgoing energy
- Have faith that your innie child will be okay and remember that not everyone needs so much socializing
- Build self-confidence based on identity rather than actions
- Give your innie child some space
- Listen to your children, both innie and outie
- Practice one-on-one conversations

If your spouse is an innie, you might remind him or her to:

- Carve out some quiet time after work
- Limit responsibilities in order to feel less overwhelmed
- Maintain energy with healthy food, breaks (thirty minutes every day), and time alone
- Find time for solitude when children are napping, resting, reading, or watching a video
- Get help from relatives, teenagers, friends, or play groups (especially if an outie child needs more outside stimulation)
- Remember that it's okay to tell your kids that you have to have time to think things over
- Accept that sometimes he or she isn't emotionally available; set the timer and request quiet for fifteen minutes
- Appreciate his or her own gifts and not try to be an outie
- Know that it's okay to not do everything your outie child wants to do
- Accept that outie kids talk aloud to think

—Zack & Josh—

Dads aren't moms who dress differently. Differences in their brains influence their behavior. If your husband is an innie he may react in his own way, different from an innie mom. Zack, an innie, spends most of his energy on his work and his family. He is quiet and shares his internal thoughts and feelings with only a few people. He enjoys watching his kids, but he tends to stand back when his extroverted partner is around. He enjoys talking with his daughter, and he finds it easier to relate to her when they are alone together.

Josh, an outie, enjoys kids that are expressive and talkative. When he is around children who are reticent and need to be drawn out, he feels uncomfortable. He loves to rile kids up by chasing, wrestling, and tickling until they are all racing around screaming. He likes to teach skills to children, especially if they pick them up quickly. He chats easily with kids but he has trouble listening. He always feels torn between work, family, hobbies, and friends. He never has a dull moment.

As you can see, temperament can shape dads' parenting styles. The more you and your spouse support your personal gifts, the better your family will function. You'll be providing a good example for your children. They will develop self-confidence if you appreciate yourself, your spouse, and your family. The example you set is the basic source of self-acceptance and healthy development for your children.

Movin' & Groovin' the Body

Exercising can be tough for many innies because they don't receive the physical rewards outies get—the endorphins, dopamine, and other chemical motivators. As we discussed in chapter 2, innies move their bodies from the voluntary side of the nervous system. They need to think their way off of the couch. It takes more effort to move. So it's doubly important for innies to find ways to motivate themselves and to land on an exercise they enjoy. They need to trigger the other side of the nervous system so they get some, but not too much, energizing oxygen and body chemicals. And even though innies may not feel immediate rewards from exercise, over time they will have more energy, sleep better, ward off depression and stress, and enjoy better health.

TRY WALKING—TRY ANYTHING—JUST MOVE

We walk in our neighborhood and our local parks. Walking is a good time for us to talk; it's ideal for Marti since it's a one-on-one situation, and it's good for Mike because he talks more in depth if he's on the move. If Marti walks alone she motivates herself by listening to mystery books on tape (she doesn't allow herself to listen if she isn't walking). Another way for innies to motivate themselves is to decide on a reward to work toward—if you keep up your exercise program for three months you can buy five new books, CDs, or videos, for example. Innies usually enjoy solo or duo exercising and individual sports. Some innies, like Marti, are physically slow, so doing group exercises or sports can be difficult. Some of Marti's introverted clients have taken up in-line skating, archery, hiking, tai chi, bicycling, yoga, dancing, snowboarding, boating, dog walking, exercising at a women-only gym, walking, golf, handball, rowing, swimming, racquetball, tennis, and karate. Innies can try any of these and others until they find a physical activity they enjoy. Schedules usually keep introverted people on track since they often don't feel like exercising. Innies need to remember to stay hydrated, eat protein and carbohydrates for energy, and take multivitamins and lethicin to build acetylcholine. Spouses of innies can provide gentle reminders to help them stay on their exercise programs.

Extroverts generally feel immediate chemical rewards from exercise and sports. They like feeling pumped. They are motivated by group-oriented team activities and gyms where they know people. Physical activities that include variety are often a hit with outies. A common stumbling block for outies is either exercising alone or falling off the exercise wagon, since they sometimes don't leap back on. Overcoming these tendencies is important because exercise or other physical activity is crucial to an extrovert's health. Physical exercise reduces anxiety, increases concentration, improves sleep, burns off calories, eliminates the effects of stress, and expands the ability to relax. And it helps to balance and burn off all of the strong chemicals outies are releasing.

Outies find it easier to schedule physical exercise into a busy schedule when they exercise with a pal or feel a responsibility to their team. Outies can ask their partners to help them stay on track. They may enjoy being cheered on or want their partners to attend their games. Marti has driven Mike's golf cart for years; she enjoys the lush, beautiful courses. Mike likes the support and he enjoys showing off his game. Mike chats with his golf mates and Marti reads. A perfect arrangement.

No-Pain Exercise Enhancers

Below we've listed a few easy ways to incorporate a little extra exercise into your life:

- Take the stairs instead of the elevator.

- Drag the trash cans in and out.

- Park farther away from the store.

- Work in the garden, rake leaves, or water plants by hand.

- Talk on your cell phone while walking.

- Get up from your desk every thirty minutes and move to improve your thinking.

- Walk around if you are looking for something; movement helps to engage the type of memory that's geared toward finding things.

- Play zippy music and dance through your chores.

- Stop by your coworkers' offices instead of e-mailing or phoning.

- Take the long way to the cafeteria or bathroom.

- Go up and down your stairs as often as you can.

- Meet a friend for a casual hike instead of meeting at a restaurant.

- Play with your kids at the park.

Head & Heart Warmers

Helping each other is one of the main reasons people partner up—two heads and hearts are better than one. Differences in values and expectations can muck up the feeling that your partner supports you. Since innie-outie couples have fundamental built-in differences, they may both feel unseen and underappreciated. Each partner wants to be acknowledged for the unique qualities they bring to the relationship.

APPRECIATION WARMERS

Most innies prefer quiet appreciation over the showy attention favored by outies. Outies usually want more strokes than innies tend to give. One way of showing appreciation that works for this type of couple is presented below. It is both subtle for innies and direct for outies. It can bridge contrasting styles, allowing each to show the other thoughtful appreciation.

Every night for a week write one new way you appreciate your partner for who they are on a slip of paper. Leave it on your partner's pillow with a little treat, such as a Hershey's Kiss. Give each other a little box or file folder to keep your appreciation notes in. At the end of the week you will each have seven reminders of the ways you are seen and appreciated. When you are feeling overlooked or unappreciated, as happens to everyone at times, take a few out and read them. Here are some of ours: "I like the way you decorated the living room. It's very warm and relaxing." "I marvel at the way you got the contractor to finish the job." "I appreciate your sense of humor."

It is reassuring to remember during busy and frustrating days that your partner notices the simple but meaningful aspects of your true self.

LOVE WARMERS

Everyone shows love in his or her own way. Everyone feels loved in his or her own way. As we showed in the story about the Brodericks in chapter 3, in which each partner had a different way of caring for a sick loved one, we all have to learn what behaviors mean love to us and to our partner.

Many innies like quiet displays of love: giving and receiving love notes, reading together, holding hands on a walk, going with a partner to an interesting lecture, making doctor appointments for a loved one, receiving flowers and e-mail cards, being listened to, and seeing a film and discussing it together.

Extroverts often enjoy dinners with friends, going to hear music, receiving a bouquet of balloons at work, and surprises. To let your outie know he or she is loved, follow the guideline often used for training adults: tell them what you are going to tell them, then tell them, and finally tell them what you told them. Outies usually don't tire of hearing they are loved. What seems like too much to an innie is just about right for an outie. So tell them that you are going to tell them that you love them, then tell them that you love them, and follow that closely by reminding them that you love them.

Showing love is an area where the different tendencies of right- or left-brained innies and outies impact harmony. Right-brained partners lead with their hearts, so they may feel loved when their feelings are considered, emotions are discussed, their partners understand what they are feeling, and those emotions are acknowledged. They may like poetry, art, emotional movies, and acknowledgment of their caring.

Left-brained folks tend to go up into their heads and show love through gift giving, physical touch, making food, doing projects together, problem solving, doing something practical for their partners, and sharing interests.

Increase your ability to adapt to each other. What behaviors can your partner do that feel like love to you? What warms your heart? What thaws your head? Gestures communicate just as much and maybe even more than words—and they are less likely to be misinterpreted. Write down a few things that feel loving to each of you and discuss them with each other. Do one for each other this week.

Let's Have Fun!

Fun is a direct path toward increasing your sense of connection and intimacy. It fires up those chemicals that shoot loving feelings through your brain and body. Below are some suggestions for you as an individual and as a couple. Please add your own favorites to the lists.

FUN STUFF TO DO FOR YOURSELF

Walk your dog, ride your bike, or do tai chi or yoga.

Read, read, read—it helps you travel inward and away from outside stresses.

Find some sun or sit under a sunlamp.

Get a relaxing massage, sit in a Jacuzzi, or take a warm bath.

Pet an animal, or go to the zoo by yourself and delight in the animals.

Help someone or volunteer at a nonprofit shelter or food bank.

Reorganize your purse or your briefcase.

Listen to music and dance around the house.

Go for a drive in a pretty area in the forest, seaside, or desert.

Stay in bed all day—don't allow yourself to feel guilty.

Smell flowers or scents that you like.

FUN STUFF TO DO WITH YOUR PARTNER

Read a book or a story to each other, using a different voice for each character.

Go window-shopping.

Buy a plant or a tree and dig in the ground.

Go bike riding or roller-skating.

Hike in the woods or walk along the beach.

Go for a long car ride and listen to music or talk.

Use children's finger paint to draw—maybe on each other.

Go out to breakfast and read the Sunday paper together.

Have a pillow or sock fight; play hide-and-seek.

Hide love notes for your partner, with clues to where to find them.

Make surprise dinner reservations at a fun or romantic restaurant.

Go play in a park and swing together.

Watch kids at an ice-skating rink.

Sit in front of a fireplace and roast marshmallows while telling ghost stories.

We Wish You Well

We hope our research, anecdotes, interviews, and personal stories will contribute to your personal and relational satisfaction. We would enjoy hearing your comments and stories. Both of us reply to all the e-mail we receive. You can contact Marti at martilaney@comcast.net or Michael at mikelaney@comcast.net. We also encourage you to visit our Web site at www.hiddengifts.net and join in the discussion forum or just read what has been posted over the years. You are also welcome to add your name to the mailing list for Marti's newsletter that usually comes out four times a year. It's chock-full of new research and subjects of interest. We also post our scheduled appearances on the Web site.

Good luck, and don't forget to value your special temperaments—they make your worlds go round. ♡

references

Beauchaine, Thomas. 2001. Vagal tone, development, and Gray's motivational theory. *Developmental Psychopathology* 13:183–214.

Bloom, Floyd, M. Flint Beal, and David Kupper. 2003. *The Dana Guide to Brain Health.* New York: Dana Press.

Brebner, James. 1998. Extraversion and the psychological refractory period. *Personality and Individual Differences* 28:543–51.

Caprara, Gian. 1994. Individual differences in the study of human aggression. *Aggressive Behavior* 20:291–303.

Connolly, Colleen. 2005. Lesbian couples: Stressors, strengths, and therapeutic implications. *Family Therapy* 4:12–15.

de Tocqueville, Alexis. 1969. *Democracy in America.* Trans. G. Lawrence. Ed. J. P. Mayer. New York: Anchor Books.

Dugatkin, Lee Alan. 2004. Homebody bees and bullying chimps. *Cerebrum* (5)2:35–50.

Golden, Bonnie. 1994. *Self-Esteem and Psychological Type: Definitions, Interactions, and Expressions.* Gainesville, FL: Center for Applications of Psychological Type.

Gould, Stephen. 1996. *The Mismeasure of Man*. New York: Norton and Co.

Gray, John. 1993. *Men Are from Mars, Women Are from Venus*. New York: HarperCollins.

Hines, Melissa. 2004. *Brain Gender*. Oxford: Oxford University Press.

Howard, Pierce. 2001. *The Owner's Manual for the Brain: Everyday Applications from Mind-Brain Research*. Marietta, GA: Bard Press.

Johnson, Debra, John Wiebe, and Sherri Gold. 1999. Cerebral blood flow and personality: A positron emission tomography study. *American Journal of Psychiatry* 156:252–57.

Jones, Jane, and Ruth Sherman. 1997. *Intimacy and Type*. Gainesville, FL: Center for Applications of Psychological Type.

Keltikangas-Jarvinen, Liisa, Joni Kettunen, Niklas Ravaja, and Petri Naatanen. 1999. Inhibited and disinhibited temperament and autonomic stress reactivity. *International Journal of Psychophysiology* 33:185–96.

Kirby, Jennifer, Donald Baucom, and Michael Peterman. 2005. An investigation of unmet intimacy needs in marital relationships. *Journal of Marital and Family Therapy* 31:313-25.

Klohmen, Eva, and Luo Shanhong. 2005. Assortative mating and marital quality in newlyweds. *Journal of Personality and Social Psychology* 88:304–26.

Kluger, Jeffery. 2003. Medicating young minds. *Time*, November 3, 30.

Laney, Marti. 2002. *The Introvert Advantage: How to Thrive in an Extrovert World*. New York: Workman Publishing.

———. 2005. *The Hidden Gifts of the Introverted Child: Helping Your Child Thrive in an Extroverted World*. New York: Workman Publishing.

LeDoux, Joseph. 2003. *Synaptic Self*. New York: Penguin Books.

Lester, David, and Diane Berry. 1998. Autonomic nervous system balance and introversion. *Perceptual and Motor Skills* 87:882.

Liberty, Kenneth. 2002. *My Partner, My Shadow.* Ann Arbor, MI: University Microfilms.

Marioles, Nancy, David Strickert, and Dean Hammer. 1998. Attraction, satisfaction, and psychological types of couples. *Journal of Psychological Type* 35:10–21.

Myers, Isabel, and Peter Myers. 1995. *Gifts Differing.* Mountain View, CA: Davis-Black Publishing.

Myers-Briggs, Isabel, Mary McCaulley, Naomi Quenk, and Allen Hammer. 1998. *MBTI Manual: A Guide to the Development and Use of the Myers-Briggs Type Indicator.* Palo Alto, CA: Consulting Psychologists Press.

Patterson, Davis. 2005. Gay male couples. *Family Therapy* 4:16–19.

Pepeu, Giovannini. 2004. Changes in acetylcholine extracellular levels during cognitive processes. *Learning and Memory* 11:21–27.

Rammsayer, Thomas. 1998. Extraversion and dopamine: Individual differences in response to change in dopamine activity as a biological basis of extroversion. *European Psychologist* 3:37–50.

Ratey, John. 2002. *A User's Guide to the Brain.* New York: Vintage Books.

Sarter, Martin, Ben Givens, and John Bruno. 2001. The cognitive neuroscience of sustained attention: Where top-down meets bottom-up. *Brain Research Reviews* 35:146–60.

Slater, Lauren. 2006. The science of love. *National Geographic*, February, 40–41.

Solms, Mark, and Oliver Turnbull. 2002. *The Brain and the Inner World.* New York: Other Press.

Springer, Sally, and Georg Deutsch. 1998. *Left Brain, Right Brain— Perspectives from Cognitive Neuroscience.* New York: W. H. Freeman and Company.

Stelmack, Robert. 1990. Biological bases of extroversion: Psycho-physiological evidence. *Journal of Personality* 58:293–311.

Swickert, Rhonda, and Kirby Gilliland. 1998. Relationship between the brain stem auditory evoked response and extraversion, impulsivity and sociability. *Journal of Research in Personality* 32:314–30.

Thorne, Avril, and Harrison Gough. 1999. *Portraits of Type: An MBTI Research Compendium.* Gainesville, FL: Center for Applications of Psychological Type.

Tieger, Paul, and Barbara Barron-Tieger. 2000. *Just Your Type.* New York: Little, Brown.

Whybrow, Peter. 2005. *American Mania.* New York: W. W. Norton.

Wolf, Sharyn. 1997. *How to Stay Lovers for Life.* New York: Dutton Books.

Zimmer, Carl. 2005. Looking for personality in animals, of all people. *New York Times*, March 1.

Zuckerman, Marvin. 2004. The shaping of personality: Genes, environment, and chance encounters. *Journal of Personality Assessment* 82:11–22.

Marti Olsen Laney, Psy.D., MFT, is a psychotherapist, researcher, author, consultant, and lively public speaker. Her first book, *The Introvert Advantage: How to Thrive in an Extrovert World*, has become nationally recognized as *the* book on introversion and has been translated into fifteen languages. Her second book, *The Hidden Gifts of the Introverted Child: Helping your Child Thrive in an Extroverted World*, has been widely acclaimed by school counselors, therapists, and parents. Marti has appered on more than two-hundred radio and television programs in America and Canada. Marti, an introvert, has been married for forty-two years to her extrovert husband, Michael.

Michael L. Laney, MBA, CPA, is a busines consultant providing organizational development, strategic planning, and advisory board-of-director services. He is certified in the Myers-Briggs Type Indicator (MBTI). He has consulted with his wife, Marti, on her book projects and was the "roadie" on each of her book tours. He has appearesd on several radio and television shows with his Marti to discuss the ins and outs of their introvert-extrovert relationship.

more **real tools for real change** in relationships
from new**harbinger**publications